TOWER HAMLETS COLLEGE
039172

ARCHITECTURE FOR ISLAMIC SOCIETIES TODAY

ARCHITECTURE FOR ISLAMIC SOCIETIES TODAY

EDITED BY JAMES STEELE

A.D. ACADEMY EDITIONS • THE AGA KHAN AWARD FOR ARCHITECTURE

ACKNOWLEDGMENTS

This volume would not have been possible without the concerted interest, concern and support of His Highness The Aga Khan, who has enabled it to be produced.

The production was directly assisted, at the Aga Khan Award for Architecture, by the staff, as well as the members of the Award Steering Committee, Master Jury and Technical Review panel, especially Darab Diba, whose illustrations are included here. I would also like to extend gratitude to staff of the Aga Khan Trust for Culture, for their help.

At Academy Editions, John Stoddart and Andrea Bettella have provided invaluable advice and guidance over the duration of the project, Natasha Robertson has shown great resourcefulness in keeping it on track, and Jan Richter deserves special recognition for his contribution to its design. JS

PHOTOGRAPHIC CREDITS

COVER: Reha Günay
PAGE 2: Reha Günay
THE MISSION AND ITS PEOPLE: Barry Iverson
VISTAS: William Porter, Christopher Little, Suha Özkan, Hazel Cook, Alex Bellamy, W Allen
ENSURING A FUTURE FOR THE PAST: Jacques Bétant, Reha Günay
COMPLEXITY, CO-EXISTENCE AND PLURALITY: Reha Günay
A SEARCH FOR MEANING: Reha Günay, Anwar Hossein, Pascal Marechaux
RESTORATION OF THE GREAT OMARI MOSQUE: courtesy of Saleh Lamei Mostafa
REHABILITATION OF ASILAH: Jamel Akbar, Christian Lignon, Claire Anne Khalil (drawing on p47)
GRAMEEN BANK HOUSING PROGRAMME: Anwar Hossein
CITRA NIAGA URBAN DEVELOPMENT: Garry Otte
GÜREL SUMMER RESIDENCE: Reha Günay
HAYY ASSAFARAT LANDSCAPING: Reha Günay, courtesy of Halim Abdelhalim, Jellal Abdelkali, courtesy of Riyadh Development Authority
AL-KINDI PLAZA: Reha Günay, courtesy of Halim Abdelhalim
SIDI EL-ALOUI PRIMARY SCHOOL: Jacques Perez
CORNICHE MOSQUE: Mohamed Akram, courtesy of Abdel Wahed El-Wakil
MINISTRY OF FOREIGN AFFAIRS: Reha Günay, Pascal Marechaux
NATIONAL ASSEMBLY BUILDING: Reha Günay, Anwar Hossain, Hasan-Uddin-Khan
INSTITUT DU MONDE ARABE: Pascal Marechaux, courtesy of Architectural Studio
THE SIGNIFICANCE OF CAIRO: courtesy of the Aga Khan Award for Architecture, Nasser Rabbat

Editorial Offices
42 Leinster Gardens London W2 3AN

Senior Designer: Andrea Bettella
Designer: Jan Richter
Editor: Natasha Robertson

COVER: This straightforward interpretation of Najdi architecture replicates the mud brick construction of the past in more durable contemporary materials; PAGE 2: Looking upward towards a skylight in Louis Kahn's Assembly Building

First published in Great Britain in 1994 by
ACADEMY EDITIONS
An imprint of the Academy Group Ltd

ACADEMY GROUP LTD
42 Leinster Gardens London W2 3AN

ERNST & SOHN
Hohenzollerndamm 170, 1000 Berlin 31
Members of the VCH Publishing Group

ISBN 1 85490 207 5

Distributed to the trade in the United States of America by
ST MARTIN'S PRESS
175 Fifth Avenue, New York, NY 10010

Printed and bound in Singapore

CONTENTS

The Mission and its People

OLEG GRABAR

Each day, over a period of three days, an unusual constellation of people emerged out of the planes arriving at the new, cavernous, international airport in Cairo. They came from Indonesia, Bangladesh, Sri Lanka, Pakistan, India, Uzbekistan, Kuwait, Bahrain, Saudi Arabia, Turkey, Iran, Iraq, Tunisia, Morocco, Tanzania, France, Germany, Denmark, Great Britain, Austria, Switzerland, Italy, Russia and the United States. There were historians of the arts, of the professorial as well as the curatorial variety, from celebrated institutions of higher learning and museums as well as from more modest institutions with relatively smaller prestige. There were also anthropologists, sociologists and scholars in other disciplines of the humanities and social sciences; from Europe, North America and Western Asia. There were British critics living in southern France, German ones from the United States, Egyptian ones from Arabia, and many from the Indian subcontinent. There were newspaper and magazine reporters from everywhere and ministers and high level administrators from France, Tanzania, Morocco and Uzbekistan. There was an interior decorator from Bahrain and an Iraqi medical doctor from New York. There were officials from many public and private international organisations. There were quite a few mere students of art, architecture and the social sciences and there were representatives of most of the major Ismaili communities from all over the world. And there was a bevy of the necessary recorders of such events: translators, photographers, secretaries, audio and visual experts who can tape and transmit what is being said and show images on a dozen screens at the same time. Accountants and financial controllers were there, ready to add up bills and expenses and to check them against budgets. There was an assortment of public relations specialists, ready to explain what was being said or what was about to happen to those in attendance and those who were not. Many of these people came with their spouses and some even brought their children. Most were relatively young for such international gatherings, as individuals under fifty clearly predominated. Women, while not in the majority, were also surprisingly prominent in the crowds waiting patiently for the appropriate checks of passports and visas at Cairo airport.

Buses brought the visitors to their hotel, a striking, tall and altogether efficient contemporary beehive around the remains of an elegant nineteenth-century palace built in connection with the opening of the Suez Canal and the first performance of Verdi's *Aïda*. The new arrivals were met there by a similarly varied array of Egyptian architects, professors, critics and helpers of all sorts. There followed a series of learned and social events, whose high point was the presentation of the fourth Aga Khan Awards for Architecture in the spectacular setting of Cairo's Citadel, suitably smartened up for the occasion.

Most of these people knew each other before meeting in Cairo, or, at the very least, they had heard of each other. Many had met before and most will, God willing, meet again. But few of them had imagined, when they embarked on individual professional careers in so many different lands, that they would eventually belong to a totally unique group, a sort of club without uniforms but with a logo, without rules of membership, practice, or behaviour but with a mission and a commitment. If it had to have a name, the club would probably be called, quite awkwardly, the 'Network concerned with the Aga Khan Award for Architecture in the lands where Muslims live and work'. But it should not have a name, just as it can never have membership cards.

For, even if it is a tangible reality every three years, when the Awards are given, and even if smaller groups from the club meet occasionally, it is less a club than a self-generated network. It arose out of a vision formulated by the Aga Khan because of his concern about the quality of the environment in Muslim lands during the early seventies. It grew, then, out of its own activities, at times for bureaucratic reasons, at other times because of the questions it was raising. The main reason for its achievement, however it is to be judged from the outside, is that its mission is unique, but, even more so, because the range and qualities of its activities and especially of the people who have devoted themselves to its continuing operation are of an order hitherto unknown in this century. I shall first turn to the character of the mission and then of the people committed to it.

There are two ways to define that mission. One is to return to the speeches and other public statements which accompanied the first Awards in 1980 and to the many papers which can be found in the proceedings of the seminars sponsored by the Aga Khan Award, in the earlier books dedicated to cycles of Awards, or in the interviews with His Highness Karim Aga Khan published over the past sixteen years or so.

From all these documents the sense of a mission does indeed emerge: to incorporate and understand the astounding wealth of fourteen hundred years of an Islamic architecture built, mostly by Muslims, for their Muslim brothers and sisters and for all of those who lived in lands ruled by Muslims; to escape from the constricting blandness of external, and mostly western, imports; to look with care, intelligence and affection at the traditional structures of the environments in which Muslims live now and have lived in the past; to find ways to adapt these structures to the contemporary world, while forming new generations of men and women ready to meet on their own the challenges of the present and, by extension, of the future and to respond to the aesthetic, if not the technological, presence of the West.

Today these words and the thoughts they imply as well as the emotions which led to them are no longer as original as they were fifteen or sixteen years ago. Partly through the efforts and activities of the Aga Khan Award, notions of architectural identity, of reliance on native rather than imported practices and talents, of an ideologically significant rather than merely antiquarian past, of technologies appropriate to each task, of new partnerships between decision making and execution, of pride in the accomplishments of the past of the lands on which one builds, of locally inspired rather than imported educational objectives in professional schools, have become standard statements in political and educational discourses everywhere.

Results may not have always coincided with expectations, but it takes time for habits to change. Yet, in theory and often in practice, considerable progress has been achieved in establishing local or regional norms for architecture, in developing critical thinking at nearly every level of planning and construction, in training young professionals to have a greater sensitivity to their past than they had previously, and in planning or designing successful works of architecture, or environmental projects in all forty-four of the world's countries with predominantly Muslim inhabitants. In a very practical sense, *the* mission or *a* mission has been accomplished. All that may be needed is to continue and to refine these new habits as new challenges and new needs creep up.

Yet, there is another way of defining that mission than by listing organisational, educational, or even creative objectives and then measuring them against accomplishments. For the cultural and political phenomena which created the original problems and which incited the Aga Khan to design the Awards that bear his name are not simple events which can be erased and replaced by new and better ones. They have deeper implications whose full understanding may well lead to a less mechanistic and more fundamental, ultimately more imaginative, definition of a mission. For, to consider change as a new revetment on the same body is to miss the depth of a problem and of an ailment whose sources lie in the history of the Muslim world.

The enormous world of Muslims in Asia, Europe and Africa and now, by the contemporary extension of these three old continents in the Americas and in Australia as well, was created by four major historical and cultural explosions, different from each other in character and by the ethnic and cultural allegiances of those involved in each one of them. These were the Arab expansion, a new faith in the seventh and eighth centuries taking over many lands with a rich past which were almost always related to classical antiquity: a primarily Turco-Mongol explosion in the twelfth and thirteenth centuries which enlarged the earlier expansion into Europe, the northern plains, and India; in the fifteenth through to the seventeenth century, a generally slower but very effective cultural, military and missionary expansion involving Arabs, Berbers, Turks of many different stripes, Iranians and Mongols primarily into Africa, Southeast Asia and the Far East; and finally the transfer, *in toto* or, more frequently, in segments, of any one existing Muslim group to almost every other part of the globe in the second half of the twentieth century. Therefore, Los Angeles or Amsterdam harbour a sampling of every possible ethnic group and sectarian faction of Islam.

The last of these expansions is, for the most part, a very recent one. It was generated by political and economic troubles in certain parts of the Muslim world and its impact on cultural matters is difficult to establish at this time. It is fair to say that it will become an important component of Muslim culture at large as well as of European and American cultures a generation from now, because its members will enter the ranks of cultural, economic and even political power everywhere perhaps except in Japan.

The first three of these expansions were almost entirely generated by internal Muslim forces and needs. They created, in different lands, a culture unified by comparison to the worlds that surrounded it, yet immensely varied in its own composition. Some of these variations derived from the earlier history of the lands involved, with continuing memories of the art of the Pharaohs, of the Roman empire, of the Achaemenids and Sassanids, or of the Guptas in Egypt, the Mediterranean area, Iran, or India, respectively; others came out of inner tensions and clashes within

Muslim culture itself (the competition between Sunni and Shi'ia allegiances, the domination of many lands by the Ottomans or the Mughals and the varying power of mystical and esoteric values). These are the centuries, roughly from the eighth to the seventeenth, of nearly all the masterpieces of Islamic architecture, from the Dome of the Rock in Jerusalem to the Taj Mahal in Agra, of all the cities, from Baghdad to Fatehpur-Sikri, which were created by Muslims. All of the cities, from Damascus to Samarqand and Istanbul, in spite of their long pre-Islamic history and often spectacular non-Islamic qualities, were radically modified by the new faith and the society engendered by that faith. And, most particularly, it was the time of the creation of several languages of architecture which all shared some features, yet were not all the same, but which, in the aggregate, created a formally recognised architectural family of its own. To some contemporary thinkers and critics the history of this lineage became independent of the history of current traditions elsewhere and grew or changed exclusively according to internal rhythms. To others, its history was always intimately connected to what happened around it, for Islamic culture alone shared frontiers with all the discrete cultures established before the discovery of the American continent, and participated, sometimes unwittingly, in the political or cultural events and the psychological or emotional make-up of western and northern Europe, Africa, and, to a smaller degree, the Sinitic world.

The contrast between these two interpretations of the history of an architecture, and culture, is not merely an academic debate for it raises the first of the deeper issues whose elaboration has become part of the mission taken on by the Aga Khan Award. That issue is whether the originality and the integrity of the great centuries of Islamic creativity derived from the maintenance, even if occasionally flawed, of a purity of single minded purpose and of an internally generated process for making decisions about the arts and the environment, or whether these very qualities are the product of remarkable powers of cultural assimilation. The will to adapt and the ability to do so creatively derive from a deep-seated certainty about one's destiny and about one's identity.

Two factors led to the disruption of these traditions which had survived so many centuries. One, which is only now beginning to attract the attention of scholars, is an internal sclerosis, the apparent inability to face up to challenges and to find solutions to internal or external problems. The other factor is European expansion which began in the sixteenth century and ended by controlling the whole planet after World War I. It includes various and at times unexpected, if only temporarily successful, offshoots such as Marxism and the Russian revolution. This expansion was politically and economically exploitative, but it was also, and for our purposes most importantly so, cultural in that it provided a ready made and pre-packaged model for living, learning and social behaviour and interaction. These models came with several doctrines, from hedonism to communism, which, on the one hand, justified these models morally and philosophically and, on the other, claimed universal values for them. Quite a bit has been written recently about these models and about the ways in which they were packaged in nineteenth-century international exhibitions in Europe and America. They still are represented in current advertisements for automobiles or electronic equipment. Beyond the packaging, the fact remains that European models in everything from clothes and cooking to buildings and art became the operative norm for Muslims all over the world.

The character and the rhythms of these factors of rupture have varied enormously from place to place and it is almost impossible to establish a unified chronology in the formation or development of either one. Nor is it important for my purposes in this essay to argue for or against any relationship between them. What matters is the apparent result: a Muslim world which has been reproducing alien forms for nearly all purposes and which did not develop intellectual and aesthetic mechanisms for making choices capable of giving authenticity to the continuing changes to the modern built environment.

Put in these terms, as it so often is, this result is indeed depressing. Something assumed to be good, a set of moral and aesthetic traditions, is replaced by something which may not always be bad but which is certainly alien. But does it have to be put in these terms? The argument could be made that all the technological advances of the past two hundred years should not be considered nor defined by the names of the lands from which they came. Microbes may have been discovered by a Frenchman, chemical tables by a Russian and X-rays by a German, but biology, chemistry, or radiology are not identified by national or even ideological labels and we all are aware of the scientific disaster which befell biological sciences in the Soviet Union when an attempt was made to do so. These changes and inventions were accidentally Western and should rather be seen as appropriate means, whatever their origin, for resolving problems of health, shelter, education and communication. Change became radical and irretrievable since that fateful moment, sometime in the early nineteenth century, when a machine moved faster than a horse, and since a more nebulous time, in the eighteenth century, when humanity overcame the religious or ethnic identification of one person. To be more accurate, neither these universally humanistic thoughts and ideologies nor the capacity to build were always used wisely and ethically. But the point has clearly been made, by ecologists in recent years, that the world cannot escape its oneness and that global solutions must be sought for human issues, just as they are for natural ones. The mission, then becomes no longer to bemoan a past which is gone, but to herald a future of common aspirations in which differences can be accommodated, but not allowed to dominate.

One can argue that this discussion should have taken place three generations ago and that it is no longer relevant to anything but a particular sub-tribe of historians who enjoy speculating on what might have happened. For in reality, since World War II, the dominant phenomenon among Muslims, as among many other cultures of Asia, America and Africa, has been the growth of the nation state and the development of allegiances to geographical entities which are very often arbitrary and whose systems of rule, varied though they are, all claim a unique quality to what they are, different from the qualities of their neighbours. At a time when electronic technology transforms almost all the mechanisms for every type of human activity into sets of formulae in a computerised expression and when almost no major enterprise can be initiated without the participation of an international financial and legal order, political and psychological allegiance is formulated and enforced, often with horrible consequences, by the ill-educated apparatus of rulers in arbitrary nation-states.

Every day the news provides examples of the deep contradictions between, on the one hand, the parochial dramas of individual cities, families and minority groups in a large city or remote area, and, on the other, the tantalising dreams and expectations transmitted by media and made possible by multi-national companies. Therein lies the third element in the mission which has, it seems to me, evolved from the activities of the Aga Khan Award: to explain and develop the practical *and* psychological or intellectual options facing humanity in the twenty-first century. Whether they are in their ancestral lands or in the anonymous quarters of enormous and varied metropolises, should Muslims seek to maintain in a new skin what their grandparents had been or should they proclaim their new identity? And what intermediary positions can be imagined?

It is thus through three directions that I can outline the deeper mission of the Award: to understand coherently and to explain in-depth the mechanisms which made a rich and very varied past appear so brilliant and successful today; to identify the ruptures which occurred in terms which would make their experience creative in meeting the challenges of today; and, finally, to ask forcefully and openly whether the narrow-minded political and ideological framework of nations should not be superseded by a generous and humane universalism.

Universal power is present whenever truly important issues or considerable sums of money are involved. It is even possible that multi-national interests, such as the arms industry, find maintaining local allegiances advantageous to their wealth. With all these issues the challenge to the Award is not simply to continue doing practically what it has done so well for more than fifteen years, which is to reward accomplishments generated outside of it, simply hoping that such rewards will become an incentive for others to continue in the same creative way. The Award should also provide intellectual and ethical direction for the century to come and to make these directions and the information and debates which led to them available to all seekers. It is particularly important to stress the notion of 'debate', since the Award has tried, on the whole successfully, to avoid doctrinaire positions on architecture and the environment and to allow for a free discussion of the issues. Yet these debates have not been well publicised, and it is easy enough to interpret the cycle of awards in terms of preferences for certain types of activities and certain formal directions over others. The Award can move to the new and challenging direction of in-depth debates because it already has access to a fascinating array of personalities.

Who are the 'people' of the Award? They can be divided into three groups which, like the organisation of ants and of bees, function with the same purpose in mind but often without encountering each other, except every three years for the presentation of awards. I shall call these groups the antennae, the 'general staff' and the heroes. There are occasionally movements between the first two categories; the last one, however, consists mostly of memories, but its importance is, as I shall try to indicate, crucial.

The antennae are the most original feature of the Award. They consist of four to five hundred individuals who are asked every three years to nominate architectural or environmental projects which have been completed and in use for at least three years. Although it is assumed, usually correctly, that most of them will nominate relatively recently completed ensembles, they are not restricted to new ones and can go back almost a generation. The Award, in this respect, differs from most prizes in that it allows for the passage of time and for the recognition that immediacy of awareness does not always mean continuity in impact. In fact, quite frequently it takes time for the true value of a work of visual art, music, or literature to be understood. Nominators are restricted to physical entities. Books, laws, policy decisions, events and teachings, which can all have enormous impact on the building of the environment, are not, at this stage, covered. But they could be and the important point is that a fellowship of people exists who, anonymously and without any personal reward (other than the right to nominate themselves), scan what is happening around them and, like so many antennae, they send out information, to those who are what I call the 'general staff'.

Theirs is a process of learning and of judgement. Individuals among them can probably be criticised for failure on both counts and it is only by experience that their errors may be found and corrected. In the meantime, the information they have provided by nominating more than a thousand projects is a unique document on the character of the building enterprise anywhere in the world and a demonstration of how the contemporary architecture of a specific cultural area has been judged by those who live in and with it. These archives are also major resources for historians, economists and sociologists, as they contain a mass of information on all the processes of building.

Another original aspect of the antennae lies in the creation and the task of a Master Jury. The Master Jury is an antenna not because it gathers information, but because it broadcasts it. It consists of seven to nine individuals chosen according to a well-established equilibrium between architects and humanists or social scientists, Muslims and non-Muslims, young and old, celebrated figures and obscure actors, men and women. Its discussions are secret and its decisions final. Unlike the nominators, members of the jury are remunerated, as it takes a great deal of time away from busy professional lives to evaluate between a hundred and fifty and two hundred submitted projects. But, even when chosen from among individuals who had been associated with the Award, they are only limited in their evaluation by their own prejudices and knowledge and by their commitment to quality in the built environment. Just as, at the beginning of the process of the Award, anonymous nominators guarantee a randomly appropriate selection, so, at the very end, an independent jury proclaims and justifies decisions about those projects which had seemed to the jury best to meet the complex and varied needs of Muslim societies.

Between the nominators and the final jury lies the 'general staff'. It consists of four separate elements. Two of them operate permanently and define the continuity of the Award. There is His Highness The Aga Khan, whose vision about the future of Muslim peoples initiated the Award, and who, with the help of his personal advisers, evaluates various possible directions for the Award, advises on its relationships with governments and non-governmental organisations, and controls its revenues. The other element is the Secretariat of the Award which is the nerve centre of the whole operation, the practical organiser of all of its activities, the keeper of its archives and the source through which information, publications, images, discussions and ideas are preserved and can be made available anywhere in the world. The other two elements are not continuous. One of these is the Steering Committee, a relatively small group of people with very different individual skills, although there too architects predominate, but with the presumed ability to see and understand the wider implications of things, with the imagination to invent new directions and with the wisdom to judge whatever is proposed. The committee's major functions are to evaluate ideas and proposals put to it by the Secretariat or by any other organisation, to initiate programmes and activities, to consider views about the future of the Award, to speculate occasionally about the feasibility of long range projects, and generally to serve as an intellectual and practical springboard for everything involving the Award. The originality of the Steering Committee lies in the fact that, since all of its members are otherwise employed and are chosen *because* of their achievements elsewhere, it can be, and often has been, the true creator of the Award's activities without being pressurised by anything other than concern for the avowed aims of the institution.

The fourth aspect of the 'general staff' is implemented during the deliberations of the Master Jury and consists of the technical review teams that investigate projects for which the jury would like additional information. Technical reviewers are usually young, they come from dozens of countries, and their reports are, for the most part, models of intelligent critical research and observation. Their data become part of the secretariat's archives, but their most important function is that they are involved in a critical root of the Award's concern, the actual operation of recently built works of architecture and the impact it is making on those who use them.

Taken together, the antennae and the general staff, past and present, as well as all those who have been singled out to receive some sort of recognition through the Award, amount to nearly a thousand men and women around the globe who have contributed to the functioning of the Award and who have learned from their participation something of the objectives and expectations of this new endeavour. There are, no doubt, disgruntled individuals, but the vast majority of them have been fully cognisant of their involvement in a novel and imaginative enterprise whose ambition is to acquire a sense of the present that is deep enough to shape the environment of the future. The dedication of all these people makes them and others like them the obvious pool from which to choose those who will ponder the questions raised by the mission of the Award and those for whom the answers to these questions will become essential as they face the twenty-first century.

But these active people from many countries and different backgrounds are not the only ones involved. The voice of those who have gone before must also be heard, since they have left their stamp on the environment and on the taste of all of us today, both in the Muslim world and elsewhere. Sometimes, as with the sixteenth-century Ottoman architect Sinan or with Hassan Fathy, the architectural prophet from twentieth-century Egypt, we know their names and a great deal about how they worked and why they accomplished what they did. At other times, as with Qavvam al-Din Shirazi, responsible for some of the most spectacular architecture in fifteenth-century Iran, we know names and can only guess about the lives behind the names. Most of them are the anonymous masters responsible for the humble constructions of small villages or of private houses, for designing whole cities, and for supervising the building of grandiose mosques, secluded fortresses, public baths, schools and wonderful palaces. We cannot ask them questions, but we can learn about their buildings in ways which almost compel a reconstruction, or at worst an evocation, of their presence and of the reasons for their decisions, as scholars and critics try to explain some unexpected detail or some forceful statement. We will not always be right in imagining the motivations behind their decisions, but we can penetrate into their creations and become satisfied that whatever it is that we understand about them is a reasonable approximation to what actually happened. Slowly and often with considerable effort, we can transform these obscure masters into the heroes of our mission. Just like the heroes of classical legends and myths, they will be present in contemporary thinking through their works rather than in person. They will not necessarily be models whose creations should be copied as exemplary individuals who knew how to solve the problems of their time, and it would not be proper to limit this category of heroes to those responsible for the traditions and masterpieces of Islamic architecture in the past. Great past masters of western architecture, such as Le Corbusier, Frank Lloyd Wright, and Louis Kahn, designed, built and taught in and for the Muslim world. They too are part of that heroic past, architects whom I have mentioned, but political and cultural leaders should be included as well, who have shaped the intellectual and the emotional make up of all who are involved in the Award. They also suggest by their involvement in the new projects of emerging nations what is also implied by the presence of so many Muslim professionals and intellectuals in the non-Muslim world which is that the oneness of the world is far more real than the differences between us and that knowledge and quality transcend boundaries.

These considerations seem far removed from the nostalgic recollection of Cairo and yet, as the images of the lines of passengers at the airport come back to me, the real conclusion to emerge is that nothing is impossible for the variety of talents, knowledge and competencies that appeared then. The institution that made it possible for all of them to gather possesses within itself the means and the structures to meet all the informational, intellectual and ethical challenges involved in understanding the built environment throughout the world and in improving the setting of life. Its proclaimed responsibility is limited to the world of Muslims, but anything that improves the environment for one fifth of mankind is bound to affect the rest. Thus we return to what I see as the fundamental question of our time: how can one preserve, in dignity and with success, separate identities, when technology, ecology, economics and the media all tend to homogenise their impact and their control? Should one even try? Few forums are more able to think about these issues than the real but invisible one that constitutes the Aga Khan Awards for Architecture.

The courtyard of the Sultan Hassan Mosque in Cairo

Vistas

CHARLES CORREA

The architect who builds a glass tower in the middle of the Arabian desert will justify the design with a hundred different reasons – except possibly the real one, which is the unconscious attempt to recreate the mythic imagery of what is perhaps the quintessential city of the twentieth century: Houston, Texas.

Such is the power of the mythic image – and the control it exercises on our lives. And this of course is the key issue at the heart of the Aga Khan Award for Architecture. How can architect and client free themselves from this colonisation of the mind? The task is not easy, nor is it one that concerns only the Islamic world. On the contrary, it is an arena in which every architect dwells, including those who build in the western world, where the dichotomy between the Modern movement and Post-Modernism, or between either of them and the Deconstructivists, can be perceived as analogues of this paradigm. Thus the agenda of this Award is really quite central to our profession; and not just the exotic Disneyland hothouse that many assume it to be. Indeed, working on the Steering Committee has provided an insight into many of the most crucial questions that confront architects here in India, as well as in other parts of the world. This essay addresses some of those issues, and the perspectives they have generated.

Mythic Imagery

To begin with, the power of mythic imagery is of course much older than Texas, it is one of the basic mechanisms involved in the design process. Every architect has an assortment of images on which to draw during the design process. Islam provides a particularly rich reservoir of such imagery. As it came out of the desert and spread eastward through Yemen and India and westward to Morocco and Spain, it brilliantly internalised the various architectural systems it encountered, integrating them into a language which is unrivalled for sheer lyrical beauty in the history of architecture. Certainly these typologies, based on the hot, dry climate which prevails from Granada in the West to Delhi and Agra in the East, generated the kind of built form which appeals immensely to our contemporary sensibilities: clusters of courtyard houses, closely packed together, sheltering each other from the sun, around large-domed public buildings built of thick heat-resisting walls.

For most people, these are the images of Islamic Architecture that spring to mind. Yet, ironically enough, the majority of Muslims do not live in countries where this kind of built form is relevant. They live *east* of Delhi; in fact, east of *Calcutta*! They live in Bangladesh and Indonesia and Malaysia. They live in hot humid climates. What they need is not dense massing, but light free-standing structures and cross-ventilation. So what is the relevance of the great domed mosque of Isfahan to them? In their part of the world, they cannot build masonry arches and domes; they must instead use sloping tiled roofs in order to keep out the heavy monsoon rains. What should *their* mosques look like? Right now, most Muslims deal with the problem by building a tiled-roof structure and then sticking a small tin dome on top (often just a flat two-dimensional cut-out) to symbolise what their effort is all about. Can the Muslim architect in Indonesia or Bangladesh be free of such images or accept them as an essential part of the imagery of faith?

Yet, is that a fair question? After all, a symbol cannot be made to order as and when we want, like a piece of clothing. Its power and meaning slowly accrues, down through the centuries, and cannot be changed overnight. Thus the Cross of Calvary is but a machine for putting people to death, therefore in nations around the world where it has been replaced by the guillotine or the electric chair, should Christian churches follow suit? Or more pertinently, can they?

Deep Structure

To answer this question, let us start by examining the way an architect designs. At work everyday in a somewhat banal world, the architect faces quite commonsensical problems dealing with clients who have particular requirements, budgets, time schedules and so forth. Within these parameters the architect tries to arrive at suitable arrangements of built form.

But at another level, just below this surface, architects – at least some of them – seem to have access to that world of compulsive, near-mythic, imagery which we have just been discussing. These images act like powerful elixirs, transforming the dross of everyday construction into something far more vivid and exciting:

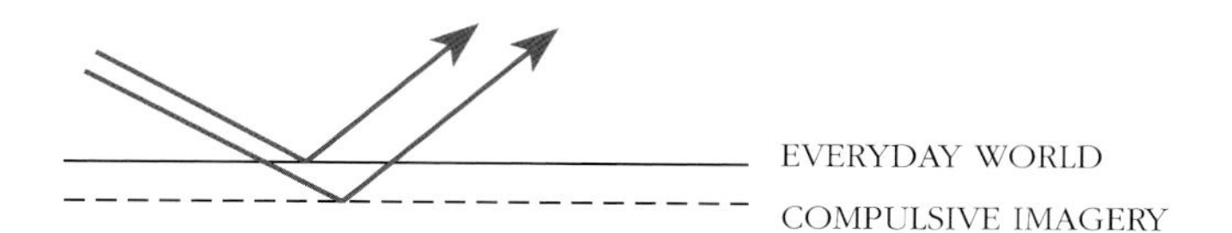

But is this the whole picture? Surely the very existence of the 'grab-bag' implies the presence of a third stratum: a far more profound deep structure, which, throughout history, has nourished the arts.

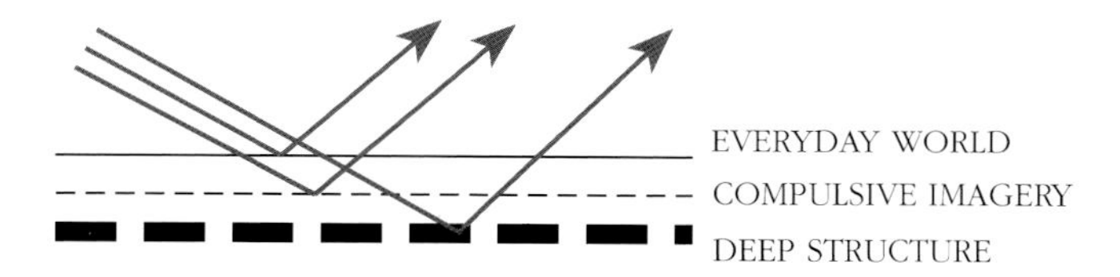

This deep structure is the wellspring of architecture, a primordial force that underlies the middle level and generates its compulsive imagery. For example, Frank Lloyd Wright created his Usonian houses not by raiding the middle level (ie the existing Tudor and Cape Cod vocabulary), but rather by his intuitive understanding of the *aspirations* of middle America in the Midwest. In other words, his path seems to cut right through the middle layer, penetrating to rock bottom mythic images of Usonia. Deposited at the middle level, they become accessible to architects and developers, forming the new lifestyle of most North American suburbia throughout this century, two steps up to the dining area, the carport, the picture window, the open plan and so forth.

Regionalism

In the process, Wright challenged the cultural elitism of America's East Coast establishment and its Beaux Arts clones. Because of the nature of their mandate, architects are sensitive to cultural bullying. Thus when asked to build the US Embassy in India, for example, the architect may try to design an 'Indian' looking building that will fit into the context of Delhi. On the other hand, if asked to design the Indian Embassy in Washington, the same architect will probably come up with a design that conveys Indian cultural values, and not American ones. So we do not really perceive these twin tasks as mirror images of each other. Both our responses are biased, but not symmetrical. We vaguely suspect that in the power struggle going on around the world, there are those cultures which are 'underdogs' and those that are 'bullies', and that the imbalance has nothing to do with intrinsic cultural value but with economic clout.

FROM ABOVE: Distant view of Houston, Texas Downtown, taken in 1988; Sana'a Yemen, 'Yemen: brilliantly internalised'; indigenous architecture, while seemingly modest, has a subtle richness that reveals itself through careful study

Hence the great emphasis among architects today on regionalism; which, in itself, unfortunately, is not a panacea since regionalism in architecture can come about in two quite different ways. The first consists of those designers who bounce off the middle layer. The main difference between them and the so-called 'International' stylists is that their 'grab-bag' of images is somewhat more localised. But essentially, it is the same superficial process.

On the other hand, there is another process, quite different from the first, that also generates a regional architecture, expressing strong cultural roots. This process involves reaching the deep structure in the lowest layer. It is a far more difficult but far more rewarding path. Such architecture does not merely *transfer* images (whether of local or foreign origin) but *transforms* them, by re-inventing them.

To understand how this happens, we must examine the forces that generate architecture. The first of these is, of course, culture. This is like a great reservoir, calm and continuous, changing only very gradually over the years. The second is aspirations, which is dynamic and volatile. It is very different from culture, though of course they interact continuously. Thus while some aspirations can be quite ephemeral, others may become an integral part of culture.

All the arts are profoundly affected by shifts along the axis that runs between these two forces. Thus if we represent a piece of architecture we all admire (for instance Registan Square in Samarqand or Chartres Cathedral in France) by a central point in a schema, then we can diagram their relationship in this manner:

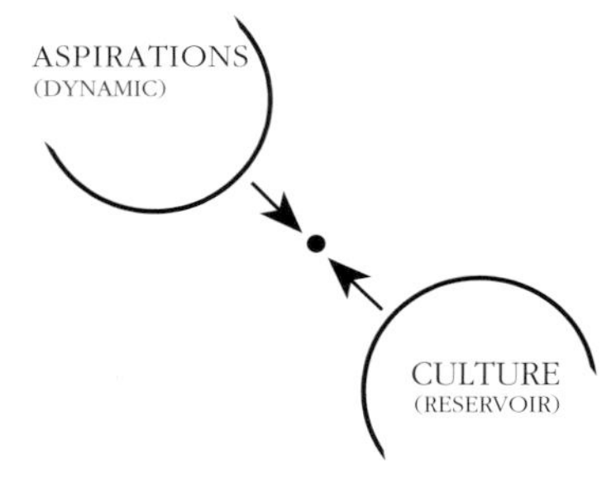

There are two other forces that exert a far more primary influence on architecture than they do on any of the other arts. One of these is climate. This is a fundamental and unchanging force. The architect must learn to master its practical implications (sun angles, wind directions, etc) and go much further than this. For at a deep structure level, climate conditions culture itself, its expression, its rites and rituals. In itself, climate can become the source of myth, as witness the metaphysical qualities attributed to open-to sky space from Mexico to Arabia and from India to Japan.

The fourth force acting on architecture is technology. No other art feels its influence so directly. Musical instruments change, but only gradually. In architecture on the other hand, the prevailing technology changes every few decades. And each time this happens, that point in the centre of our diagram moves to a new position:

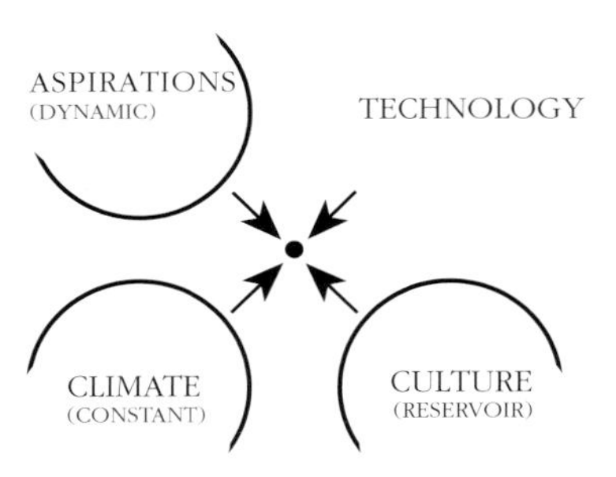

Architecture comes into being at the point of resolution of these four forces. Sometimes this point moves because of a shift in the basic cultural paradigm. This happened in India when the Vedic concept of architecture as a model of the cosmos was replaced by the sacred values and imagery of the Islamic Garden of Paradise, which in turn was overrun by the arrival of the Europeans with their mythic belief in science and rationality. In European history, the change from Romanesque to Gothic is probably the expression of a change in technology, but that from Gothic to Renaissance is clearly the fall-out of a decisive shift along the cultural-aspiration axis.

Transfer and Transformation

Changes along this cultural-aspiration axis are shared by architecture with all the other arts, many of which, such as poetry and music are indeed much purer arts, since they do not have to deal with the exigencies of the pragmatic and commercial world we live in. No, it is the frequency and decisiveness of the *technological* changes that are unique to architecture, and that make it such a sensitive barometer of the health and robustness of a particular society. This is why cities, and the buildings they contain, are of such decisive importance to the cultural historian.

For when we have to substitute stone with steel, or wood with concrete, we are faced with a challenge: we can either use the new technologies to superficially *transfer* the old images (hence the fake Gothic arches and Islamic domes, that we see all around us), or we can *transform* them, re-inventing the architectural expression of the mythic values they represent. Both options work, but there is a difference. The process of transfer is facile but debilitating. Transformation, on the other hand, challenges society and renews it as well. This is the challenge, and the reward, that architecture represents in society every time the technology changes.

A prime example, in our own century, is the work of Le Corbusier. Each one of his projects is the work of 'un homme méditerranéen', yet none uses a sloping red-tiled roof. What Corbusier did instead was to *re-invent* the Mediterranean ethos in twentieth-century materials. Similarly in North America, the work of Louis Sullivan and his colleagues in Chicago generated the energy which has fuelled US architecture for a century or more. But the modus operandi of Post-Modernism (looting the middle layer of 'Wham-O' imagery) has weakened that same society because, at a fundamental level, it provides no nourishment.

The Sacred and the Banal

Thus through recognising the value of architecture which is regional, we can address issues which are universal. For all true architecture is, by definition, regional. Not because it retreats into a Disneyworld of facile imagery (History as Caricature), but because it expresses those prime forces (culture, aspiration, climate) through using the technology available at that particular point on our planet. In this profound sense, all the finest examples of architecture in history, from Fatehpur-Sikri in Agra, to the temples of Nara, to the Oak Park houses of Frank Lloyd Wright, are all regional. Not because they exploit the superficial layers of facile imagery, but because they make contact with the deep structure that lies beneath.

For it is through this process that architecture expresses the sacred invisibilia that underlie society. By sacred, one, of course, means not only that which is evoked by religion, but also by nature, by the primordial and the mythic. The Japanese tea ceremony and the bull fights of Spain are but two examples. These obviously deal with elements buried deep in our subconscious, such as the riveting centrality of a house around a courtyard. To cross the hot desert plain and arrive at such a house is an experience beyond the merely photogenic. Something deep is stirred in our mind – perhaps the memory of a lost paradise?

In this layer of invisibilia lie the roots of architecture. Perhaps this is what Louis Kahn was referring to when he spoke of his yearning of the non-existent Volume Zero of History. 'Architecture' he said 'deals with the recesses of the mind. With that which is not yet said, and not yet built.'

In this context, are Islamic domes eternal symbols of a religion, or accidents of technology? If the latter, then perhaps it might be better for the architects of Bangladesh to search in a deeper stratum of mythic intuition, as for instance, the Koranic Garden of Paradise. How can the Char Bagh be expressed anew in the lush tropical climate of Bengal? Perhaps from such questions may arrive the architecture they seek, an architecture which, at one and the same time, is both regional as well as universal.

In this search, we should be open to new technologies, whenever appropriate and available, keeping intact our own self-confidence. When, and why, does a society pause mid-stride and doubt itself? The matter is indeed a delicate one. In the early eighties, when they started drinking Pepsi Cola in China, one sensed instinctively that this was going to be the beginning of the end, that eventually all of Mao's China must unravel. On the other hand, when you see New Yorkers eating in a Chinese restaurant, do you panic and think that this is the first step in the Chinafication of America?

The difference of course is one of self-confidence. When Islam came out of the Arabian desert and spread towards Iran and Yemen, it was full of confidence in itself. It found wonderful architecture which already existed in these places, which it just absorbed, ingested, made its very own. Thus when Islam arrived in India, it discovered all kinds of exotic marbles and precious stones which it had never seen before, and these again were assimilated and internalised with great self-confidence. And so we get Agra, Fatehpur-Sikri, Mandu and many other masterpieces. And we get the stunningly beautiful housing typologies we find in the hill towns of Yemen and the wind-catching houses of Iran, all of which, regardless of origin we identify today with Islam. Where has that self-confidence gone today?

Housing and Habit

This brings us to another range of issues with which the Award is vitally concerned, and which is also of fundamental importance to much more than just the Muslim world. These are the issues which concern our housing, our cities and our environment.

The building of the habitat we have just been discussing, as everywhere in the world, is an organic process, involving society as a whole. The incredibly beautiful houses in Mykonos, Rajasthan and Tahiti are not the brainchild of individual architects, but the product of the entire community and its history. For people can indeed produce the housing they need as naturally and instinctively as birds build nests. In fact, habitat which addresses just about every one of our contemporary concerns (balanced eco-systems, recycling of wastes, human scale, cultural identity and so forth) *already exists* in the vernacular building systems of people throughout the world. What does *not* exist is the urban context where these solutions are viable. This then is our primary responsibility: to help generate this context.

This is why we must always pay the keenest attention to efforts that attempt to provide the support structure, the subsystems, which generate habitat. This is of crucial importance to urban centres, not only in the Third World, but increasingly in the industrialised nations as well. As our cities decay, the situation worsens. Those who suffer most of all, of course, are the poor.

How can the architect, using professional skills, help in this process and not simply express a feeling of compassion, like Florence Nightingale among the wounded? The answer is by not acting like a prima donna professional, but more modestly and anonymously. It is a role which has very important precedents. Throughout Asia, and elsewhere in the world as well, the architects' prototype was the site *mistri*, that is an experienced mason/carpenter who helped with the design and construction of habitat.

The extraordinarily high quality of these master artisans is evident not only in housing, but also in the architectural masterpieces of history. In fact, without these peerless craftsmen, the Taj Mahal and Fatehpur-Sikri would have been an impossibility; not only in their construction, but in the very conceptualisation of the architectural language itself. By totally undervaluing the decisive contribution of these craftsmen to architecture, we have, over the last few decades, discouraged them to the point of extinction.

Our arrogance stems from a lack of understanding of architecture and its relationship with the other arts. So we design a building and then put some art into it, or a piece of sculpture in front of it, which is indeed myopic. A mural need not just adorn a room, it can, through the tension it generates, totally change the dynamics of the space. This is what the frescos of Fra Filippo Lippi do to those courtyards in Florence, or the cave-paintings in Ajanta do to the landscape without, or, for that matter, the white and golden cherubs of the rococo churches of Austria, flying in from the windows, beckoning in the daylight. It is important that we understand and clarify in our minds the roles of the various players such as builders, architects and clients, involved in the creation of architecture and why sometimes it succeeds, and why sometimes it fails.

The Processes of Architecture

This is indeed an important question. When one looks at the architecture in the countries around the Gulf, one is aware of the incredible mismatch between the high quality of the architects who were commissioned for the projects and (in far too may cases) the low quality of the results. Why does this happen? It is irrelevant that a number of the architects involved are foreigners. On the contrary, when the city of Chandigarh in India was being designed by Le Corbusier forty years ago, many people wondered: don't Indian architects object to this key project being assigned to

FROM ABOVE: View along the side of the facade of Frank Lloyd Wright's Robie House; cupola fresco by Damiam in the rococo Weltenburg Abbey Church; the use of local red sandstone makes Fatehpur Sikri seem to blend with its surroundings, particularly at dawn and dusk

a foreigner? I always replied: No, on the contrary. We are lucky to get Corbusier. He takes architecture very seriously. We can only profit by his example. This indeed proved to be true; in two important ways. Firstly because Le Corbusier's work was at the cutting edge of architecture, and India suddenly moved to centre stage as the focus of attention for the whole profession. People came from all over the world to see Chandigarh and Ahmedabad. Far from feeling they were working in some weird corner of Disneyland, Indian architects felt part of the mainstream and still do today. Secondly young Indian architects had an extraordinary opportunity to learn from Le Corbusier's architecture.

This was indeed true. Not only did young Indian architects learn from his extraordinary buildings, but also from exposure to the man himself. His contract with the Government of Punjab stipulated that he spend a month on site in Chandigarh, twice a year. This was in addition to his collaborators Pierre Jeanneret, Jane Drew and Maxwell Fry, who resided there full-time on contracts which lasted several years. Thus the interface with India (and with Indian architects) was considerable, and mutually beneficial. We had in-depth access to creative processes of the highest order. At the same time, being exposed to the climatic and living conditions of the Punjab was of immense benefit to Le Corbusier not to mention the feedback from the users of his buildings.

This arrangement was not unique. In their design of New Delhi in the twenties the contracts of Edwin Lutyens and Herbert Baker stipulated that they reside continuously for six months a year in Delhi for the duration of the project. This was of decisive importance to the success of the venture, since it allowed them to absorb a far more vivid understanding of the country, its climate, its culture and its people.

In contrast, most architects in the Gulf get by with a kind of parachute planning and designing which is quite horrendous. They fly in for a few days (or hours) on projects much larger than Chandigarh. What is their exposure to the locals? And vice versa? It seems clear that there is (or should be) a difference between architecture and carpetbagging. And the clients should be astute enough to understand this. They must not only insist on a far more lengthy interface, but they must also take an intelligent interest in what the architect is trying to achieve. If they don't, then they have only themselves to blame.

No building can be better than the architect who designs it, or the contractor who builds it, or, one could add, of the client who commissions it. This is where the rich clients around the Gulf have some soul-searching to do. Years later, reading some of Corbusier's writing from the thirties, in which he appeals somewhat effusively to 'the Captains of Industry', one suspects that all he may really have been trying to do was solicit for clients – who, luckily for him, did not swallow the bait. If the Gulf Boom had occurred in the thirties, Corbusier might well have got involved – and ruined – in the process. As I said before: India was lucky to get Corbusier. But he, too, was lucky to get India. Here he met clients who believed in the seriousness of architecture, and what it could do to our lives.

Coda

I can never forget the brilliant address that the scientist and humanist Jacob Bronowski gave at the summation of the 1967 Aspen Design Conference on 'Order and Disorder'. Computers were then the newest buzzword among architects and designers, and there seemed to be no end to the wonders they would achieve. Bronowski took a less optimistic view. He illustrated this by examining the old proposition that 'a monkey pecking randomly at a keyboard would, sooner or later, type out the entire works of William Shakespeare'. Bronowski was sporting: he took not the whole works, but just the sonnets; and not all the sonnets but the celebrated one which starts with:

Shall I compare thee to a summer's day?
Thou art more lovely and more temperate.

In fact, Bronowski took only the first two lines – and showed it would indeed take a great deal of time to finish these two lines by random selection, even if the monkey were to by replaced by the fastest mainframe computer. Bronowski gave us his calculation for each consecutive word, but when he reached the last word of the second line, he stopped and said: 'You know, any of us would know that this word must have three syllables – but only Shakespeare would have thought of this extraordinary word: temperate'. To Bronowski, neither Art nor Science is the product of random action. As he put it: 'If Nature wants to produce honey, it first produces the bee. If Nature wants poetry, she first produces Man.'

So perhaps when Nature wanted the exquisite architecture of the Alhambra, she first produced the Muslim. For when we look at the incredible range and beauty of Islamic Architecture down the centuries, are we not also looking at societies who through the elimination of sculpture and painting and the reliance on calligraphy, through the non-availability of tensile materials and the reliance on masonry vaults and domes were meant to produce architecture of an incredibly high order? Not just the great architects who are justly celebrated in history, but also more humble practitioners. To return to those standards, might it not necessitate an analysis of that programming, and its re-invention in the context of the aspirations and technologies of our times?

Ensuring a Future for the Past

RONALD LEWCOCK

'Time, not man, makes architecture' *(Garcia Lorca)*. This line, written by a great Spanish modern poet, explains why, for many people, prolonging the life of buildings is an important part of the work of the contemporary architect.

One of the best justifications of the specialised skill of the architect is that he or she makes possible the continuation into the future of valuable qualities of the environment, form, texture, material, and of detail and decoration, that would otherwise disappear. By signalling buildings and towns for special care, the architect distinguishes them from their fellows, emphasising their potential to serve the ends Lorca proposes for them. But this skill also has dangers. Since the action of time on buildings is judged to be an important factor, it does not do to rebuild them, to create pristine forms and details, to replace the patina of age with spanking new materials and textures, to put newly carved decoration in the place of old. Too much acknowledgement of the contemporary would defeat its own purpose. This poses a dilemma for the conserver of individual buildings, and even more for the conserver of urban areas.

In including the category of architectural conservation as part of the Aga Khan Award, the organisers were concerned with two problems that seemed endemic to the countries of Islam: firstly, that many buildings in Islamic countries were neglected and in a state of disintegration. The second problem is that some attempts at conservation, regardless of the best intentions had failed. It was not uncommon to see buildings on which considerable sums had been spent less than a decade before, again falling into disrepair.

So in premiating conservation as one of the aspects of the Aga Khan Award, the organisers wished to focus attention on projects which had developed conservation strategies, that promised to be successful on every level, and might therefore be studied as models for other projects.

In the case of individual buildings, success was found to be primarily due to three factors. The first of these is research into the true causes of deterioration in the structure and materials. The second factor is the respect for the principle of using, as far as possible in the conservation work, the original building materials and craftsmanship. Only if this were done would weathering soon cause the repair to be invisible, and the natural ageing process of the whole building be allowed to continue uninterrupted. The third factor is the caution taken in the use of new materials. That is, to study the consequences of their physical and chemical interaction with old materials and their different weathering properties, such as cement, plastic and aluminium.

The three conservation projects which received Awards in 1983 were all individual buildings, but each had a strong contextual component. The Shah Rukn-i-Alam tomb in Multan has historically dominated the city from a site high on the former citadel. Its dilapidated state, before conservation was undertaken, had a depressing effect on an ancient but vital city of craftsmen and artists.

The Azem Palace in Damascus occupied a historic site in the ancient souk area close to the great Omayyad Mosque of al-Walid. As the largest accessible private dwelling in the historic centre, a focus for the revival of arts and crafts as well as a museum of traditional culture, its deplorable condition had become a symbol of decline in the old city.

The third project was actually intended by its sponsor, the German Archaeological Institute in Cairo, to have a direct impact on urban rehabilitation in the old city. By selecting for conservation five historic buildings in one traditional quarter, it hoped to provide for the people of the neighbourhood an exemplar that would encourage them to undertake the renovation of their own houses. It was thought that such a seed planted in the old city might grow and spread to other areas. Here, the conservation work was initially undertaken by an architectural historian, Dr Michael Meinecke, who achieved remarkable success with the first building to be renovated, the Madrasa al-Anuki. Subsequently, a young architect, Philip Speiser, joined the project and, after Meinecke's departure for Syria, completed the projects. The work of this team was characterised by the great care taken to locate and use the last of the master craftsmen surviving in Cairo, and by the willingness of the architects to learn traditional techniques and use them wherever possible. It is notable that the money received from the Award was itself used to undertake another major conservation project adjoining the earlier work, the renovation of the Madrasa of Mohammed Nasr.

The impact of the Cairo project proved to be both encouraging and disappointing. The restored buildings, hitherto derelict, were generally put to use by the local inhabitants or the authorities. The two religious buildings became mosques which now actively serve the community. But the impact of the five conserved buildings was not seen to affect the condition of the remainder of the environment. There were a number of reasons, both local to the quarter and generic to the old city, to which this may be attributed. Absentee ownership, prevailing poverty disputes between neighbours all contributed to mitigate against the spin-off effects of improving the major monuments. But a significant factor also seemed to be the feeling that the conservation work was done by and for foreign tourists and therefore it was not ultimately judged by them to be a concern of the people of the neighbourhood. A salutary lesson, nevertheless, but the conservation work of the German Archaeological Institute remains some of the best renovation work of its kind ever done in the old city of Cairo, an inspiration to all on how much can be achieved on very low budgets to conserve at least some of the architectural masterpieces from the great ages of Islam.

The conservation of the Shah Rukn-i-Alam tomb in Multan was undertaken by a senior architect, Walli Ullah Khan, who had already distinguished himself with the conservation of the Badshahi Mosque in Lahore. In advanced age, and with a pair of younger assistants, he undertook the works of conservation of the tomb, which had developed a major split due to the movement of its foundations and was generally in an advanced and ugly state of dilapidation. In preparation for this work the Awqaf arranged for the restoration of the surrounding fort wall by other authorities, and this work has unfortunately proved to be faulty. The tomb itself was conserved by Walli Ullah Khan in an exemplary fashion, using traditional techniques almost exclusively. A major effort was made to locate craftsmen who understood the ancient techniques of tile making, and even more importantly, to locate sources of the mineral deposits for the unique coloured glazes of the original tiles. An aged descendant having been found of the family who originally made tiles for the tomb, six hundred years before, it proved possible to revive a craft which seemed completely lost, and to restore the unique heritage of the decoration of the tomb in all its original glory, to the way it must have looked in the fourteenth century. This work was preceded by the most painstaking reconstruction and strengthening of the original structure and repair of its brickwork. Although the tomb has been so thoroughly restored that some of its patina of age has been lost, the great achievement of the conservation project was twofold: major medieval craft industry in Multan has been revived and continues to flourish, and the tomb today is revealed, for the first time in centuries, as one of the great achievements of Islamic architecture on the Indian subcontinent.

FROM ABOVE: Aerial view of Old Mostar, which has regrettably now been destroyed due to civil strife; the eighteenth-century Azem Palace is one of the masterpieces of Damascene architecture – showing the intricate stone banding on the facade; the inner dome of the Al-Aqsa Mosque, Haram al-Sharif, Jerusalem, with painted motif; OVERLEAF: A view looking north along the main street of historic Cairo, named after the Fatamid ruler al-Muizz li-Din Allah, looking towards the sabil-kuttab of Abd al-Rahman Kathuda, one of the seven structures restored as the first phase of the Darb Qirmiz restoration programme in Old Cairo

The Azem Palace had been damaged in warfare during the French occupation of Syria. Although restored in the thirties, neglect and inadequate repairs had led to its returning to an advanced state of deterioration by the seventies. It was the love and dedication of one of the curators of the museum in the palace, Shafiq al-Imam, which then led to its successful conservation. He supervised each stage of the work and undertook the location and training of the craftsmen employed on it. The result is the return to its full beauty of one of the most magnificent examples of the legendary Damascus Islamic palaces. The Award is said to have made a considerable impact, encouraging other conservation work of the kind in adjoining areas of the old city of Damascus.

How can the old be kept side by side with the new? The answer suggests a plurality of values that only the most sophisticated will be likely to share, an attitude that will be constantly under threat in a world that advocates modernity and creative change. Even if isolated monuments may be allowed to survive in this way, like the ancient Roman temple now serving as a church in the main street of Assisi, the protection of a whole urban area does seem equivocal. It would demand adjustments to an individual's expectations of the environment, and to the community's attitude to functioning of the city and would require a strong consensus to succeed. So far, only in extreme cases, such as Venice, has a majority been prepared to sacrifice its expectations of the urban environment and forfeit its dependence on the car.

The first project for the conservation of an entire old city centre to receive an Award was that of Mostar in Yugoslavia in 1986. Here, one man, Dzihad Pasic, who had formerly been a regional conservation officer, took the initiative, by forming an organisation, Stari-Grad, which persuaded the municipality of Mostar to waive taxes and concede control of services in a small area on either side of the famous single span bridge crossing the Neretva River. While the buildings and streets were being brought back to the appearance they had a century earlier, the bridge itself was thoroughly studied and conserved. The demonstrable success of this first phase made it relatively easy for Pasic to persuade the authorities to grant him the same opportunities in a further thirty buildings surrounding the first zone. The enthusiasm engendered by this phase in visitors and townspeople alike enabled him to further extend his operations until, at the outbreak of civil war, the entire area of the seventeenth-century town was part of the conservation scheme. By conserving, renovating and in a few cases reconstructing the old commercial and residential buildings of the town, Stari-Grad was able to finance conservation work on streets, services and public monuments. This demonstration of the self-sustaining ability of urban conservation was unfortunately brought to an end by the conflict in his country, with Mostar suffering more damage than many other centres. It is to be hoped that the strong condition to which the buildings had been returned will have reduced the damage they might otherwise have received, and that the example of Stari-Grad's work will inspire the eventual restoration of Mostar and many other towns like it in that country.

Also given an Award in 1986 was the conservation of one of the most hallowed shrines in the Islamic world, the Al-Aqsa Mosque adjoining the Dome of the Rock in Jerusalem. The Award initiative stressed the restoration work on the dome of the mosque, which had deteriorated to such a degree that water leakage had effectively obliterated the valuable painted decoration on the inner surface. All this was saved, the roof reconstructed, the paintings returned to their former brightness and the work extended to encompass the whole of the rest of the mosque and the structures of the gates and fountains of the Haram beyond. Encouraged by the Award, conservation of the great building of the Dome of the Rock itself is now being studied.

As part of the 1986 Awards, honourable mention was made of the work of the Touring and Automobile Association in Istanbul in conserving a number of historic buildings, many of which had been pavilions in royal parks. In addition, the Touring Association undertook the conservation of large numbers of old timber houses in two areas adjoining historic monuments. The first is around the Kariye Camii, where it also repaved the streets, restored the local fountain house and conserved a major teaching school of the seventeenth century for use as a craft school. The second area lies between the Topkapi Palace and Hagia Sophia, where the conserved and reconstructed houses will be used as hotels and one as a library of the Association.

Urban conservation involves tackling public institutions, those organs of society and of government that control the structure of urban life, up to the very highest realms of authority. To do this the architect has to take on a new responsibility, to persuade the heads of these institutions that their hard-fought goals and standards may be abandoned in the very places where the battle began, the old urban centres, to allow values to survive that they had always thought should be swept away. No wonder that urban conservation, if successful, is a slow business, involving long and patient campaigns to enjoin the general public and government officials alike to appreciate the values of their own cities and to accept willingly the need for strategies to protect and preserve them.

Implementing urban conservation brings the architect into unfamiliar collaborations. Keeping a traditional urban area functioning traditionally and yet in step with modern times, as far as sanitation, services and ease of access is concerned, means working with teams of experts in water supply, drainage, sewerage, road and public transport design. The need for amenities involves the architect with electricity, telephone, television, ambulance, fire-fighting, school and medical planning, to name but a few. Among the myriad decisions that have to be made are the types of paving in the streets that would blend most suitably with the traditional environment, whether there should be sidewalks to protect pedestrians or not and if they may be out of character with the old area, if motorised vehicles should be admitted at all and if so, whether this access should be limited to certain times of day.

In addition, there are also questions of how to reverse immigration out of the old areas and coping with social change; of improving the economic base of former city centres so that they may continue to be self-sustaining; of relating the new urban areas to the old; of dealing with the plurality of lifestyles and of dealing with the specialised and unusual transportation systems that such conservation projects may need if they are to be successful.

The Fourth Award Cycle

The urban conservation of a coastal town in Morocco, Asilah, resulting from the enthusiastic initiative of leading members of the local population, received an Award in 1989. To achieve this, attention was first drawn to the small town by the establishment of an Arts Festival in 1978, which eventually became the most celebrated and heavily attended festival of its kind in Morocco. Using incentives brought in by this success, the initiators were able to obtain backing for the improvement of the infrastructure and services in the town, and for the restoration of the major buildings. Thus encouraged, many citizens embarked on the private conservation of the old houses in the town. Eventually, one of the principal activists in Asilah became the Minister of Culture in the government, and was able to participate in the presentation ceremony of the Award representing his country.

A second Award in 1989 was given for the conservation of the Great Omari Mosque in Sidon, which had been severely damaged during fighting in Lebanon seven years before. The conservation work was judged exceptional in its attention to the qualities of the original building, and the Award Jury particularly drew attention to the value of this project as a model in resisting the widespread tendency to tear down buildings damaged in the war in Lebanon and replace them with new structures.

The Aga Khan Award is continuing to draw attention to the importance of the specialised aspect of the work of architects that deals with the care of old buildings and urban areas. In addition to devoting some awards to conservation, the Award is now involved, through its parent organisation, the Aga Khan Trust for Culture, in a Historic Cities Support Program in aiding the international attempt to achieve these goals.

Islamic buildings were generally built on the assumption that they would receive continual maintenance. The advanced decay now threatening many of the buildings and towns of the Islamic world is of serious concern to everyone who admires the extraordinary level of human achievement that they represent. The situation is similar from Morocco to Indonesia. The issues are generally the same and the conflicts and problems are often exactly duplicated. Only by making enormous efforts to save them, with singular clearness of purpose, determination and the development of specialised skills, is there any chance that this heritage can be preserved into the future without the loss of the unique qualities that were celebrated by Lorca.

Complexity, Coexistence and Plurality

SUHA ÖZKAN

Modernity and tradition as two diametrically opposite perspectives in life have substantially occupied the intellectual agenda of the present century. Modernity, following in the footsteps of industrial revolution, has sought continuous change, a better future, wide distribution of amenities, an aesthetic of plenty and other attributes related to the times. Interestingly it found a strong basis of existence in both liberal and authoritarian societies as it has politically formed an appealing future to enable many to have access to global resources. In the widespread and over-powering presence of modernity, traditionalism has kept a very low profile. Nevertheless, it has always been present in almost every society with a particular mission to maintain certain values which were in danger of being lost to change. In the case of our present century, such change has inevitably responded to the demands of modernity.

In fact modernity has been an over-arching ambition for many nations, not only as a political ideal, as it has been formulated by many powerful leaders since the end of World War I, but also as a new way of life. After World War II the societies of both the East and the West have witnessed the massive destruction of their cultural and architectural heritage in order for the 'new' to replace it. This process of replacement has favoured the 'newer' as well as 'the modern' version. Technology and mass production have provided so many different solutions for old problems that to ignore their contribution would be synonymous with foolishness. The total system of our immediate environment has changed with the provision of conveniences like: heaters, refrigerators, cleaners, washers, closets, etc . . . all of which did not exist in the traditional way of life. Furniture has also been transformed as the habits of the people became 'modern'. The buildings as shells containing these functions could not be an exception. Since architecture possessed the great power of reflecting life-styles, they transformed faster than any other. Therefore architecture has been caught in the changing idiom earlier than many other aspects of life. The final consequence of this change may more appropriately be regarded as the demolition of what had existed at a gigantic scale.

In the cities of the Third World, where the population pressure has been enormous, there have not been expansive new areas with the infrastructure necessary to establish the new buildings which would accommodate new lifestyles. To provide that infrastructure meant vision and planning and more cost to the investors or the public sector. So it was ignored. The sad option was demolishing the old and building the new on the same land where the amenities existed. Modernity – or change – inevitably and unnecessarily became a pretext for destruction. Consequently, when the excitement subsided, it had to be blamed for such destruction. Obviously this did not have much to do with Modernism, its teaching or ideology. Regardless of modernity, the so called conveniences have brought so many other problems into urban life, that in a very short period of time, what was referred to as modernity collapsed. The causes for the failure were not simple, and had few identifiable apparent determinants. They were manifold. Vocal traditionalists who had been intellectualising the anti-modern discourse did not hesitate to blame modernity for everything that went wrong. When they were a small minority the media did not pay attention. Due to increased public concern, the media found the traditionalist discourse interesting and joined them to incriminate Modernism. Not at the large, societal scale but in the realm of architecture and planning, the failure has been due to incompetence, lack of insight, concern, vision and talent. As these were complicated to deal with, certain segments of the media have preferred a simpler message. The polar dichotomy of the *modern* and *traditional* was soon invented, and manifested itself in the urban form. It needed more time to be visible as it had more subtle undertones, which emerged in other aspects of life.

There is another aspect of Modernism worth dwelling upon which is its claim for universality. In the sixties many philosophers were speculating a global culture in which the mass media values, and the medium of communication would share and develop. When these discussions were taking place satellite television was not known and video tape was a rare commodity only affordable by professional studios. The eighties witnessed a shrinking world where conscience and culture were also to be shared globally. The phenomena of various news and entertainment networks became the reference sources of a global information flow. The new values and realities of information and entertainment became a part of the global network. In addition to this, the local networks reinterpreted or redistributed these broadcasts, which eventually reinforced and widened their influence. This occurred in spite of rather worrisome questions like: Who owns the media? Who decides on the priorities? Who benefits in the end? Nevertheless, the factual correctness of their content as well as repetition secured their credibility. The competition for others to join in, guaranteed control. This brought plurality into existence allowing people choices. Dramatic changes in the eighties occurred as political camps collapsed and a longing for a more universal and perhaps more homogenised world emerged, all owing to the influence of the media. The information flow that had been monopolised by newspapers and was exclusively available to literate and multi-lingual elite became accessible to the general public via telecast media. Global networks have gained power by transforming local issues into global ones. All local events regardless of being political, cultural or climatic became material for wider distribution and global consumption. In return, what used to be global became of local concern. As famine in Sudan became an international priority, the hole in the ozone layer became a local subject. Global awareness anticipated in the sixties, became reality in the eighties.

The cultural implications of this new information flow and its network are complex. They definitely deserve attention as the sensors and communication patterns of an emerging culture. It is also essential to note the power that this network has on our global existence, dictating the values of our natural and built environment. What is very interesting is the two way action of the emerging global communication network. As it projects values of the universal global existence it has to go to the local scene to generate material for the interest of the wider public. Therefore new information is simultaneously injected into the media to be shared by all. Be it cultural, political or natural the seeds of coexistence are sown by the same information flow.

However abstract it might have been, globalism began to occur in the field of architecture as early as the nineteen-twenties and thirties. When Modernism became the *lingua franca* of architecture and design, it gained the power to express and strongly reflect many aspirations of contemporaneity, regardless of geography, history or culture. With its high regard for advanced technology, mass production, honesty of expression and the materials associated with it, this tendency has increased since then. Modernism is now conceived as the equivalent of 'global' and traditionalism has become 'local'. In the meantime, serious concerns have arisen about the role of architecture, not as a reflection of extremes but of daily life. The design language which has reflected the 'global' has been 'modernity'. It has, conceptually, close association with being 'in touch with the times', international, and all the subsequent associations with universality. The other pole of 'traditional' values has been referred to as being local, contained and related to the conservation of the historical continuity.

In architectural theory Modernism had unrivalled hegemony until it was challenged by counter movements like post-modernism, Classicism and traditionalism. At the present time architectural discourse is characterised by a tendency of duality. Two lines of thought coexist, which each deny the relevance of the other.

Between global and local polarities the pendulum of concerns has now swung in a rather confusing arc. What has been intellectually and professionally rather unhealthy has been the lack of dialogue between the proponents of the extremes and the accusative nature of the discourse. Traditionalism and its derivations have cast Modernism in the role of villain, responsible for the ills of present day urban and environmental chaos and disaster. Modernists, in defence have labelled their attackers as the ones without a sense of future, retrogressive escapists from reality. Modernists are portrayed as the aggressive transformers of the environment and the traditionalists as romantics who demand nothing but a peaceful life of the kind that existed before the industrial revolution. Architecture, as the melting pot of all cultural expression, has shared in this polarisation and become ideologically charged. In fact, the ideological conflict between traditionality and modernity may not exactly be seen as being manifested in modern or traditional architecture. But, the undertone of the ideological discourse is pervasive and architecture and urban planning are exceptional in this regard.

The widely advocated failure of Modernism has brought traditionalism to the foreground as an alternative solution. Many architectural theorists, especially from the mid-seventies onward, diagnosed traditional built environments, which grew and matured over the course of a long period of time with the participation of all aspects of the society as a remedy for all. Was it possible to revive tradition? Was Modernism the sole cause for environmental deterioration? In time it became clear that there is no clear answer to either question because time has taken its toll and society has transformed the basic relationships between society and production. The built environment is only one reflection of these relationships. Modernism has never been the cause but has only indicated the way in which to cope with the relationships between technology and urban society. On the contrary established Modernism has certain ethical principles in order to deal with the problems of plenty. A serious search of the issues behind environmental deterioration has not been undertaken. Certain facts have now been formulated in a rather simple, axiomatic form. The apparent causes for such problems are now considered to be the following: existence of the cultural values in the built environment; continuity between the past and present; a sense of identity; consideration of climate and a need for user (or community) participation.

When His Highness The Aga Khan established his Award for Architecture, in very broad terms these were the issues which had been substantially disregarded by the architects who were consequently held responsible for creating an inharmonious environment. His concern was primarily for the Muslim World which was dramatically neglected. In retrospect the last twelve years show us that the Award has been the only institutional, discursive platform where a genuine search was undertaken to explore solutions for our times by enhancing the cultural content that would restore meaning and depth to people and environment. The Aga Khan Award for Architecture has situated itself in the centre of this debate with the broadest possible theoretical base. In its search, the Award has not categorically rejected the possible relevance of any approach. By doing so, it has ventured to benefit from both modern and traditional lines of thinking as well as other variants.

Similar to the difficult tasks facing any institutional building process, the difficulty lay in establishing the intellectual integrity and value of the Award. A philosophy had to be instituted and a direction needed to be defined. During the lively debate that ensued the Award found itself in a position where the realities of the future, demanded by modernity, were as important as the values of the past and the sense of meaning as offered by traditionalism. The two lines of thinking had to be synthesised. The issues were defined through a critical process of thinking organised in the form of seminars, think-tanks and publications. Priorities were examined from the point of view of their content, understanding of lasting values and deep social concerns. In this process, modernity provided important aspects such as orientation towards the future, recognising the importance of technology, along with industry in offering comfort and convenience through mass production. All of these are undeniable features of our lives in the contemporary world, and yet, tradition has its roots in an indefinite history and cherishes continuity, meaning and community. The Award has always endeavoured to re-establish the ruptured link with the history without rejecting the use of the modern means and expressions.

The first two cycles of the Awards of 1980 and 1983 identified the issues, exemplified them in the solutions and signalled these issues to the wider public and the profession. With the announcement of the projects the architectural profession observed the establishment of new priorities. It also noticed that the boundaries of its profession had been forced open and redefined. The social awareness of the profession was much more visible than ever before and areas of building activity which were never thought to belong to the profession became visible. For instance, The Kampung Improvement Projects took the profession by surprise and instigated a whole new attitude.

The 1986 Jury indicted Modernism and passed a strong judgement in favour of traditionalism and populism as a remedy for the ills of modernity. By doing so the Jury confined the realm of their awards to a particular architectural ideology within which solutions should be seen to be viable. That area was the theoretical domain of Classicism, vernacularism, populism and contextualism. All of these approaches respected whatever had been existing in the society and the direction for the future was only indicated in perpetuating the theoretical lines of these rather conservative commitments. This honest, dedicated and rather strong message alarmed the profession. It began an exciting debate on the relevance of the Award and the relevance of a particular sector of architecture. The Award has benefited substantially by voicing both arguments and has incorporated them into its thinking. The level of expectation in the field of architecture of the Muslim world has now become profound as a result. In its search for solutions the profession did not like its options to be restricted to the past and to tradition exclusively. It had hopes that technology could be considered to be a viable alternative to tradition. The message of the 1986 Jury was regarded as a strong commitment, emphasising one dimension of the problem while people who were expecting direction from the Award continued to hope that they could benefit from a multitude of ideas, in different scales of complexity.

The 1989 Jury had the legacy of the three past cycles of the Award to consider. It also benefited from the heated debate of the preceding cycle. The Jury decided to address the complexity of the situation by pointing out the outstanding projects independently as examples of architectural excellence. The eleven premiated `projects cover almost the total spectrum of architecture from rural to urban, from low to high technology. The criteria of architectural excellence was flexible. The jury courageously pointed out exemplary projects at polar extremes without hesitation. Whether this was done in recognition of plurality or as a reflection of the understanding of the complexity of the situation, remains to be seen.

As global awareness has increased, the interests and concerns of people to share each others' problems and cultures have grown proportionally. To represent one's cultural achievement to another, or, to inform and influence the public of another country by means of having a presence there has a long history in the form of cultural centres. The Institut du Monde Arabe represents this phenomenon. Architecturally it reflects a symbiosis of the bend of the River Seine, a relationship with the University Campus next to it, the city of Paris and the Plaza which were all moulded into one form. By a deliberate architectural choice the Institute has been characterised as being on the cutting edge of contemporary technology, designed by an architect who has been more inspired by cinematography than any other sector of the arts. As an architect Jean Nouvel does not see architecture as a prescribed set of experiences which are designed to be experienced. On the contrary he wishes to project an episodic space-time continuum where the architecture forms the means and the context of a personal experience with space.

The survey which the Award conducted in order to determine the reaction of the Arab community in Paris to the building has surprisingly proven that expatriates (ie Muslims) living there did not want to be associated with the superficial paraphernalia or relics of their folklore back home, but wished to have a cultural presence in Paris. They felt that this presence ought not to be associated with backwardness in time. This is a very important aspiration which has been captured by the architect. Apart from the architectural qualities which merited the Award, the positive reaction of the community to the hi-tech expression was indicative of a changing societo-sphere in which a global culture has taken root. People who have been very proud of their past as well as their tradition and culture choose to take this usage for the expression of their presence in Paris. Jean Nouvel's playful hi-tech detailing, which depicted some abstract elements of Islamic architecture such as *mashrabiyya*, blended with a contemporary expression and was correct in allowing people to feel at ease with the existence of this culture.

At the other end of the spectrum, the Jury recognised the traditional approach. Abdel Wahed El-Wakil's series of mosques situated dramatically on the urban seascape of Jeddah has been a most challenging alternative to the forceful beautification programme on the embankment built on the reclaimed land which the city had used as a means of expressing a search for a distinct image and identity. El-Wakil's skilful regeneration of various forms from the architectural heritage of Islam has been justified by the history of Hijaz where every holder of this holy land brought the best from all over the world. When compared to the excessive sculpture garden on the embankment, El-Wakil's mosques are extremely distinct architectural elements and powerful symbols. The traditional content of architecture as the most expressive of all the arts in Islam reinforces El-Wakil's message. In designing these mosques he has used nothing but authentic load-bearing brick construction with white stucco finishing. Three of these mosques along the embankment create an episodic message that strengthen their joint existence. El-Wakil's mission bases itself on his diagnosis of the rupture and disconnection with tradition and the antithesis of Nouvel's hi-tech interpretation of abstract architecture elements. His approach has found a comfortable nook in the architectural discourse of the late eighties under the mantle of Classicism.

The Master Jury's recognition of the achievements of these two extremes on the scale of architectural approaches offered them the chance to span this spectrum with projects which each exemplify different aspects of the architectural reality in the Islamic World.

Three of the projects were related to the problem of context. If the young architect Samir Hamaici, with the support of the Association de la Sauvegarde de la Médina, had not intervened, a standard prototype school building would otherwise have been erected in the Medina of Tunis. The Sidi el-Aloui primary school has strong references to an architectural idiom developed by Serge Santelli in his Residence Andalous which has previously been recognised by the Award in 1983. The extremely important aspect of this is that the Award has obviously benefited from its own recognition and influence. It also provides architectural tools for architects to emulate in similar circumstances the idiom developed for the context.

A diminutive, loosely organised summer residence in Turkey which was also recognised with an Award, was seen as having the potential of becoming a generic form with its unpretentious pose, without any loud declarations. In fact it intrinsically refers to widespread building forms in the informal sector where a minimum of technology and material resources are used. The form is not a primary objective but a natural achievement in the process of unpretentious building. This house is still spatially rich and rather sophisticated in its configuration.

The third of these contextual projects is the Citra Niaga Urban Development Project in East Kalimantan, Indonesia. The project is contexually conceived from both the social and the architectural points of view. Precious urban land which was occupied by street vendors was developed by making use of these vendors as the initiators and eventual beneficiaries of the final scheme. From the phasing point of view, the project has a more profitable part such as the small apartments which were built in the early phase to finance the rest of the project. The project architects were also concerned with urban reality and responded to it by offering more public space to the city than before. In a short period of time a project which was conceived within the frame of reference of current market forces and urbanistic ideas has added to the quality of life in East Kalimantan.

The understanding of unobtrusive architecture well placed within an urban or natural context was exemplified by these three projects. Obviously none are great masterpieces of architecture but rather timely solutions with a great potential to be replicated. Two additional projects considered by the Jury are the Al Kindi Plaza by Ali Shuaibi and the Beeah Group and BBW, with Richard Bödeker as designer of the Diplomatic Quarter Landscaping. The former re-invents an urban structure which relates itself to an architectural heritage related to the desert structures of the Najdi culture of the Riyadh region, redefined in contemporary material and construction techniques.

The Diplomatic Quarter Landscaping project takes the dialogue with nature to its extreme and successfully attempts to re-discover the plant species that survived in the hot arid climate of the region until recently. It uses them for the greening of an extensive desert landscape ecologically known to be deprived of any vegetation. By doing so not only is scarce water saved but also the earth has been developed to hold its own humidity to generate top soil in the years to come. It is an attempt to regenerate more liveable landscapes on our planet.

These projects were followed by two major buildings which constitute a new generic type not addressed by the Awards earlier. Henning Larsen's Saudi Ministry of Foreign Affairs building is a subtle exercise in modernity which seeks to establish roots in a society where traditional ties are strongly sought. He has achieved this in a very abstract manner by allowing the culture of the desert to reflect itself in modern architectural form. Components of the building, such as the corridors, relate to the traditional souks or to streets in medinas; openings to *mashrabiyyas* and traditional Najdi windows. However all do so abstractly without any clip-on pastiche. The Parliament building, which was designed by the late Louis Kahn, initially intended as the capital of East Pakistan then became the same for the State of Bangladesh. This masterpiece is a product of Kahn's most mature period when he began to explore the richness of forms and novel expressions for large scale buildings. The Assembly Building has acquired the power to symbolise a nation with a population of more than one hundred million which takes pride in it.

The architectural mastery which shaped Sher-e-Bangla Nagar has already been historically acknowledged and the Award simply followed suit. Very interestingly, this building, which is probably one of the largest in the world, was accompanied by a rural housing project which is unique. The Grameen Bank enables the rural population in Bangladesh to accommodate themselves much better by allowing them to have access to credit facilities and to obtain some building components in order to bring an element of safety and sanitation into their shelters. These are simple pre-cast columns and toilet units designed for this particular culture and climate. The rest is left to the individual families' creativity. The outcome of providing $3-400 credit to each family has been stunning, providing tens of thousands of homes for the most deprived sector of Muslim society.

The last of the Awards recognised a mosque which is a monument to the understanding of plurality in its own history. The Great Omari Mosque has a superstructure which is the remnant of a Crusader Castle dating from the twelfth century. The Mamluks erected a mosque on top of this Castle in 1291, which was subsequently destroyed by the bombing of Sidon. Though the community had the chance to build an entirely new structure, they chose to restore the old mosque.

The 1989 Awards reveal the present plurality of forces existing in today's Islamic world. The buildings range from the lowest to the highest possible technology, from the classical to the modern, from the smallest weekend residence on the Aegean to a huge parliament building in Dhaka. The message they convey reflects the complexity of the situation; one must never expect simple, standard recipes. With this the Jury challenges the indoctrinated version of Modernism which claimed to standardise solutions. With the same rigour the Jury also disagrees with the theory of Classicism in the present sense and with neoclassicism in the nineteenth-century sense since the problem is not one of technology and form exclusively. The solutions instead have to be a culmination of many factors expressed in architectural form.

In the projects that follow, the Jury has selected examples which have specific relevance to a particular problem or context. In doing so it has chosen to address specific questions, such as the problem of landscaping in a hot arid climate with minimal or no irrigation, or rural housing with minimal financial input and the problems of identity and expression of Muslims living in the West. In addition to these it was also able to identify architecture of quality in each and every project.

FRONTIS: The painted patterns surrounding the fenestration of the Yemeni house reflect light and glare away from the interior

A Search for Meaning

JAMES STEELE

When His Highness The Aga Khan established an award for architecture, it was intended to both increase public awareness of Islamic culture and to create a forum for examining the appropriateness of contemporary architecture throughout the extremely diverse community of Muslims worldwide. Since 1980, this award has been given every three years, and in the selection process used to determine the winners, the jury has typically considered the particular context in which each project has evolved, as well as the unique social, economic, environmental and technical factors to which it responds. In looking back over the successful projects of the past, there is a consistent pattern of appropriate and creative utilisation of available resources in meeting functional and cultural needs, as well as the higher potential in each project to set a standard for the future. The Aga Khan acts as the Chairman of a Steering Committee that governs the Award, and the term of this committee spans each three-year cycle. Its task is to oversee the distribution of prizes totalling $500 thousand that are awarded in each cycle to projects selected by an independent Master Jury. Those awarded include architects, construction professionals, craftsmen and clients who are considered most responsible for the final realisation of each project.

In the fourth Award ceremony, held beneath the towering walls of the Mohammed Ali Mosque on top of the Citadel in Cairo on October 15th 1989, a strong feeling of continuity and confidence emerged making it a turning point in retrospect in the history of the event.

In his introductory remarks, His Highness The Aga Khan noted that, perhaps more than any other time in the past, there had been a special awareness of the tripartite contributions of restoration and preservation, social and community development and the search for what he called an 'architecture of quality' in their turn, which has continued to highlight the important role of each in suggesting valuable directions for the future of Islamic architecture.

In recognition of the deeply felt need to preserve historical monuments that represent the best architectural traditions of a glorious past, an award was presented to those involved in the restoration efforts on the Great Omari Mosque in Sidon, Lebanon. Dating back to the Bahri Mamluk period, the Mosque was erected in 1291 on the remains of a castle built by the Knights of St John during the second Crusade and the buttresses on its southern facade still reveal its use as a fortress. Many additions and improvements were carried out during the late Ottoman period, ultimately presenting a mosque based on a central courtyard plan enclosed by four *riwaqs*, or porticoes. The prayer hall itself is located in the southernmost *riwaq*, which is covered by cross-vaults. In addition to severe weathering, the Mosque suffered extensive damage during the Israeli invasion of Lebanon in 1982, to the extent that a local patron named Rafiq al-Hariri offered to replace it with an entirely new building. The local residents refused to give up the old mosque, however, which had always served as both the physical and psychological centre of their community, and requested that it be restored instead. While restoration and preservation efforts have been cited by the Award in the past, and have included monuments of such importance as the Al-Aqsa Mosque in the Al-Haram al-Sharif in Jerusalem, the circumstances surrounding the destruction and precise rebuilding of this mosque have given it a special significance.

Another award, given to the municipality of Asilah, has recognised community efforts of an entirely different kind, involving the rehabilitation of a small town on the Atlantic coast of Morocco. Two local men, named Mohammed Benaïssa and Mohammed Melehi, came back to Asilah after graduate studies abroad and determined to improve their town. The highly personalised way in which they did so really began with the question of how the innate creativity of a community can be marshalled for positive change. The first steps they took in attempting to answer that question are an object lesson in the effectiveness of straightforward tactics that have now served as an inspiration for other such communities throughout the world. They began by organising a small cultural festival in the town in the summer of 1978, which attracted nearly one thousand visitors from the local area. This modest event gave the townspeople a renewed sense of civic pride and self-worth that has continued to grow as rapidly as the festival itself, which now attracts nearly 125,000 people and is one of the biggest cultural events in the Middle East. The overall rehabilitation of the town has also encouraged many private individuals to build new houses in the traditional manner throughout the fabric of the medina, to replace others which had deteriorated beyond the point of possible restoration.

The Grameen Bank Housing Programme, a further Award winner, has successfully attempted clever innovation of another sort, based on a concept that has already challenged past theories of how to assist in providing self-help housing for the poor throughout the developing world. As the first of two schemes to be given in the social development category, the Grameen Bank Project has been implemented in Bangladesh, which is one of the poorest and most populous countries in the world, where nearly fifty per cent of the rural population is both landless and homeless. The basic concept as initiated by Mohammed Yunus, who is the managing director of the Bank, has been to offer small loans of the equivalent of $350 to the rural poor without requiring any collateral, in direct contradiction to the customary reluctance of the financial community to do so in the past. In his view, every human being, regardless of social position, deserves a life of dignity and should be given the opportunity to care for himself if possessing the commitment to do so. Personal commitment, then, becomes the main criterion in determining credit worthiness, and not financial resources. With these small housing loans, each borrower is provided with a pre-fabricated concrete slab, four concrete columns and twenty-six corrugated metal sheets for a roof. The pre-cast building materials are mass produced and made available to the borrowers at very low prices. The residents build their houses themselves, typically enlisting the help of all of the members of the family to do so, in order to keep costs low. The end result is a unit that usually consists of a rectangular, twenty-square-metre area, that is dry and sanitary. Whatever else the inhabitants want to include is usually added on an incremental basis. It has now been more than a decade since the programme has been in effect, and hundreds of thousands of Bangladeshis have benefited from it, with more than forty-five thousand such homes in existence. With a pay-back rate of nearly ninety-eight per cent during this time, the Grameen Bank, or 'rural peoples' project has also demonstrated that institutional changes must precede any significant progress in housing for the poor.

The second social improvement scheme to be honoured in the series was the Citra Niaga Urban Development plan for Samarinda in East Kalimantan, Indonesia. In comparison to the wide ranging institutional implications of the Grameen Bank initiative, the major achievement of Citra Niaga is the lesson it offers in the effectiveness of the self-controlling system of cross-subsidies that were used. A democratic management board represents the interest of the local government, as well as the shop keepers and street peddlers, and both the equity and the benefits have been shared by all three. This project has totally transformed a former slum area, which had previously been occupied by low-income, migratory settlers, into a well planned urban and commercial complex. The programme that has achieved this transformation has been implemented in three stages, concentrating primarily on a commercial development, which was sold to finance the second stage related to the informal sector. Smaller shops, to be offered for sale, were built in the third phase. As built, the centre is now made up of two hundred and twenty-four stalls that have been provided without cost to the street peddlers, as well as two hundred and twenty shops of various sizes that are incorporated within a series of arcades that cater to medium and high income shoppers. The public spaces, which include such amenities as a covered podium for entertainment, give the centre a lively character, and traditional roof forms create a feeling of unity between the different components of the complex. This project has not only achieved its social and economic objectives, but has transformed Samarinda into a vibrant and well-designed urban centre.

The remaining seven project to receive awards in Cairo, which varied in scale from a modest private home to a National Assembly building, all represent the intangible quality of architectural excellence deemed so important in setting a standard to be followed in the future throughout the Islamic world.

The Gürel Residence, in Çanakkale, Turkey, clearly reflects the concern of architect/owner Sedat Gürel, with having the house blend into its surroundings. In this area of the Aegean seacoast, the design required sensitivity to both the steep, rocky slopes that angle down to the water, as well as the dense groves of pine, olive and oak trees that cover the site. The residence is a cluster of seven units, distributed over the site in direct relationship to a long wall that protects them from the road nearby. The pavilions consist of two living units, four sleeping areas, and one common service element, that are arranged along the wall in such a way that open-air courtyards are created between them. The overall feeling of the house, which uses local domestic construction techniques as well as indigenous forms, materials and details, is that of a small scale traditional village, which promotes the special qualities of the site by providing private as well as communal spaces. The ingenuity used in juxtaposing built elements and open areas, as well as the use of simple, local construction methods, makes this house a logical model for a variety of locations.

In contrast to the private retreat created by Sedat Gürel, is the Al-Kindi Plaza in Riyadh, Saudi Arabia and the Hayy Assafarat landscaping scheme, which address public issues of the appropriate character of communal spaces, in this case within the contemporary Arab city. The Diplomatic Quarter, where these twin projects are located, is the final realisation of a long-held wish of the Saudi government to consolidate all of its political and administrative functions in its capital city. The central area of the quarter is a curving, one hundred and fifty metre wide strip of land that is intended to contain all of the public, community services for the area, which are distributed along its twelve hundred metre length. Al-Kindi Plaza itself, which is named after a famous Muslim philosopher, has been designed by Saudi architect Ali Shuaibi. It contains a Friday Mosque which can accommodate up to seven thousand worshippers, as well as residences for the Imam and Muezzin of the mosque, a library, a government service complex which houses the Riyadh Development Authority, and shops surrounding a central maidan. In deference to the traditional Najdi architecture of this region, the buildings are designed with central courts, and thick, insulating walls that present small openings to the outside. Both the buildings and the open spaces also reflect Najdi decorative patterns, and huge entrance gates located along the main boulevards provide access to the central maidan. As Shuaibi has said in regard to his design of Al-Kindi Plaza:

> This project attempts to demonstrate that many of the problems faced by post-industrial architecture stem from the destruction of the context into which a new building might fit. Once this context is re-created, good design can easily follow. We emphasise that valuable architecture is that which the pedestrian can appreciate, and that the quality of the built environment results essentially from the entire fabric, including the variety of open spaces that are the result of the structures surrounding them. Local traditions, in the shaping of climatic and cultural environments, should not be abandoned in favour of mechanised technology because there really is no contradiction between the two.

The question regarding the re-use of traditional forms and decoration reawakened a controversial issue that has run through all of the past cycles and has yet to be resolved. This question has been particularly sensitive because of the rampant and uniformed application of 'Islamic' decoration on a majority of the recent export architecture throughout the Muslim world. This has resulted in what Professor Dogan Kuban of Turkey has called a misplaced reliance upon a kind of 'cultural fetishism' that blindly uses forms from the past without a full understanding of their mean-

FROM ABOVE: Stairs and woven rush siding are ways in which inhabitants have personalised their homes in the Grameen Bank Programme; beige stone approximates the appearance of the earthen architecture that once identified the area; the mechanised mashrabiyyas; *FRONTIS: Covered bridge leading over the artificial lake surrounding the Assembly Hall*

ing. The ongoing debate between those who advocate the use of such forms as a model, and others who seek to renew the processes that produced such forms so that they then might be used as a reference, surfaced again when the Sidi el-Aloui Primary School in Tunisa and the Corniche Mosque in Jeddah, Saudi Arabia, were presented with awards. The Sidi el-Aloui school is one of twenty projects that were initiated in 1983 to rejuvenate the Bab Souika-Halfaouine district of the medina of Tunis, and is located in a tightly-ordered district with many older structures in it. The school is sited on the northeast side of a rectilinear public park, and houses sixteen classrooms distributed symmetrically around two internal courtyards. The main entrance is on an axis with the public park that faces it, and is made obvious by the large *mashrabiyya* balcony that projects out over it from the first floor. While seeming somewhat insignificant from a western viewpoint, the use of such detailing on this public building represents a major victory in Tunisa, where it had once been considered frivolous. This courageous exploration of traditional forms, as both a necessary and economical alternative to standard governmental proposals, presents an example of great value to other developing countries.

The Corniche Mosque in Jeddah is by Abdel Wahed El-Wakil, who has been cited by Prince Charles in his book, *A Vision of Britain*, for his tireless efforts to heal what he considers to be the destructive division now existing between the architect and the craftsman. In this building, which has brought El-Wakil a second award following the award for his Halawa House, given in 1980, the architect is intentionally literal in his use of a traditional language, in a continuing attempt to find the missing link between the rich inventiveness of the pre-industrial age and the tenuous relationship between craftsmanship and architecture today.

The Corniche Mosque is only one of a series of mosques requested by King Fahad Ibn Abdul Aziz, and supervised by the Ministry of Hajj and Awqaf as part of a national programme to develop a contemporary mosque architecture in Saudi Arabia based on more traditional models. The Ministry, in collaboration with the Municipality of Jeddah and Mohammed Saïd Farsi, who was the Mayor when the project was begun, chose several high visibility sites around the city for new models of traditional mosque architecture. In addition to providing places of worship, all of these models were intended to exhibit methods of traditional construction, and to show that buildings using these methods were achievable on a limited budget. To do so, conventional ideas of glazing, as well as strict air conditioning requirements also had to be changed, which was far from easy in this hot, humid region that has converted so completely to western standards of mechanised environmental comfort. The Corniche Mosque epitomises the spirit of the entire programme, emphasising the perceived importance of sculptural form as a means of enhancing the image of these structures in the contemporary urban scene. The design of this mosque is compact, yet manages to be full of intricacy. A strong directional pull from exterior to interior is set up by the compositional interplay between the dome over the prayer area, and the vault covering the main entrance, which El-Wakil has extrapolated from the Mamluk mausoleum of Umm Anuk in Cairo. After entering, this direction is continued and further refined by allowing screened views to the sea through selectively placed windows and an arcade.

Prior to entering the prayer hall from a narrow opening on the left end of the vault, the full height of the minaret comes into view through an open slot that separates the main dome over the prayer hall, and the two smaller domes covering the loggia-arcade beyond. The strong visual impact of this minaret, leading the eye upward to the sky, is a dramatic prelude to the peaceful seclusion and meditative quiet of the prayer area itself, which is the final goal of this carefully orchestrated sequence.

The issue of the re-interpretation of historical forms was also of deep concern to Danish architect Henning Larsen in his design of the Ministry of Foreign Affairs in Riyadh, Saudi Arabia, which received an Aga Khan Award. As a result of the same consolidation effort that created the Hayy Assafarat and the Al-Kindi Plaza, the project Ministry organised a competition in 1975 for the construction of a new Foreign Ministry and invited twelve world-class firms, including Renzo Piano, Arata Isozaki, Ricardo Bofill and Kenzo Tange, to participate. The generative idea behind the concept that Larsen developed is that of a 'hidden', inward facing architecture which is closed to the outside world, but slowly reveals itself from within. This idea of internalisation is further articulated by insulating the triangular public courtyard that he has created in the centre of the building from all of the private office spaces on the perimeter with a semi-public internal 'street'. As the concept developed, each of the corners of the symmetrical triangular form were expressed as nearly separate entities related to the three programmatic divisions of political affairs, cultural and economic affairs, and administration and finance that exist within the Ministry.

The entry to the building is flanked by elements that are common to all divisions and thus comprise a fourth 'zone'. There is a public reception hall here with a one hundred and fifty seat auditorium and a seventy-five thousand volume library, which is under the auspices of the

Diplomatic Institute, and is primarily stocked with books on the history and development of nations and diplomacy, as well as having its own bookbinding capability, rare manuscript division and slide library. The Foreign Ministry also participates in a 'Mahad' programme in which post-graduates throughout the kingdom can enrol in a two-year course in diplomacy, and this library-auditorium zone is the self-contained sphere of activity for this programme.

The monumental image of the building is intentionally meant to be reminiscent of the older, Najdi style of Riyadh, specifically the massive walls of the historic Musmak Fort nearby. Larsen has chosen to extend the thermal advantage of these thick walls by introducing an intermediate cavity that acts as both additional insulation and a source of light. His double wall diffuses the direct glare that would otherwise enter through the small punched windows he uses, and absorbs much of the heat as well. Larsen speaks poetically about the quality of light entering his building, and of his intention to make it a 'sundial', which would track the progress of the day on its interior walls. In the inner world that he has created, nuances such as this, as well as the exquisite materials underfoot, take on added significance. His abstract, yet fundamental reading of this particular regional architecture, in this case, treads a careful path between the vernacular features of the Najd, on the one hand, and more international forces on the other, that is meaningful to each.

Light, of course, also had mystical qualities for architect Louis Kahn, and was one of the most important considerations in his design of the National Assembly Building in Dhaka, Bangladesh, which was honoured with an Aga Khan Award. In the same way as Larsen, Kahn has also recognised the need to control the full glare of the sun in a region in which direct exposure can be fatal. Like the Ministry of Foreign Affairs, the National Assembly Building is monumental, and transcends merely functional requirements in order to institutionalise democracy in a nation that has had its fill of strife. While some have criticised the building as being far too lavish for such a poor country, Kahn has succeeded in giving the people of Bangladesh a national symbol to be proud of, as well as a feeling of self-worth that is beyond price. Unlike Larsen, Kahn did not copy elements of regional architecture, but has submitted to the specific local conditions and construction patterns of Dhaka. The result is a building that is both universal and place specific in its expression.

The same may also be said of the Institut du Monde Arabe in Paris, which is precisely fitted to the curve of the left bank of the river Seine, near the opening of the Boulevard St Germain, and is divided into two sections that are separated by a square central court. The curved, scimitar-like section facing the quay contains exhibition halls and a museum of Arab art and civilisation, while the second, rectilinear block, which makes the transition to the orthogonal city grid behind it, houses the library. As a cooperative effort between France and twenty Arab countries, the building really does represent what architect Jean Nouvel has called 'a dialogue between cultures'. In its precise and polished modernity, the Institute is an appropriately urbane Parisian building, constantly offering a reflected commentary on its surroundings; and yet also presents many tantalising reminders of a more obscure sensibility. In addition to the pristine calm of the open central court, or the cross reference between the spiralling 'Tower of Books', and the famous minaret of the Mosque of Samarra, the most perceptive of these is the contemporary and technologically brilliant rendition of the traditional wooden *mashrabiyya* screen used throughout the Middle East as a device for controlling sunlight and privacy in the past. The southern facade of the Institut is clad with over a hundred photo-sensitive panels, containing nearly sixteen thousand moving parts, that act like the diaphragm of a camera in controlling the amount of sunlight coming into the interior of the building. Photovoltaic sensors electronically adjust all of the moving parts of these panels, which are made up of a polygonal openings that echo Islamic geometric forms.

In spite of several questionable aspects in its design, the Institut du Monde Arabe has managed to fulfil its intended purpose, and has brought about an increased awareness of Islamic society within the city as well as establishing the cultural bridge it sought to build. Because of this major achievement, as well as its ingenious hi-tech transformation of traditional elements, the project is most certainly deserving of the recognition it has received.

The completion of the fourth cycle, concluded a decade of searching and questioning, and the Aga Khan Award for Architecture seems to have come of age. The wide range of awards presented demonstrates the characteristic of unity in diversity in the Muslim world itself, making it a more accurate reflection of the culture it seeks to explore. As the record of the fifth Cycle held in Samarkand in 1992, and presented in *Architecture for a Changing World* demonstrates, the categories defined in Cairo have now become the framework by which future Awards are calibrated. The directions taken by juries may differ from it, but it remains a definitive example by which those differences are gauged.

Report of the 1989 Master Jury

Preamble

The Master Jury for the 1989 Aga Khan Award for Architecture met twice. In January, it considered the 241 projects submitted by the Award's Nominators, and selected thirty-two to be studied in depth by Technical Reviewers. Then, at the end of June, the thirty-two finalists were reviewed on their own merits and in terms of the issues they reflect, the questions they pose, and the messages they send. The decisions which follow are unanimous, because the Jury agreed to make it so, but unanimity was not reached for every project and sharp differences remained to the end on projects which are premiated and on some which are not. Throughout its deliberations, the Jury sought to listen to all views and to feel respectful of the projects nominated as well of its own very varied opinions. Furthermore, as it discussed the nominations, the Jury became aware of needs and opportunities for the architecture affecting Muslims everywhere which had not been as fully visible in previous Awards. The differences within the Jury and the new sense of a universal Muslim community have been incorporated in four statements the Jury wishes to make before presenting the Awards themselves.

As in the past, the Jury congratulates the staff of the Award whose dedication, enthusiasm, humour, kindness and efficiency made the Jury's labour a pleasure. It also congratulates the Technical Reviewers, all of whom undertook their uniquely responsible tasks with creative enthusiasm. They have all contributed to the richness and sophistication of the information available to the Jury and stored in the offices of the Award. No segment of contemporary architecture anywhere is so wealthy in data and so well cared for.

The overall dimensions of the architecture affecting Muslims have changed enormously since the Award was created twelve years ago, partly perhaps under the impact of the Award itself. Five aspects of these new dimensions struck the Jury: better quality of the final products and of the processes leading to them; complexity of the physical, social and economic components of social and community building; fuller coverage of contiguous Muslim regions; awareness of the large Muslim communities within non-Muslim worlds and the enormous increase in the quantity and quality of nominated projects built by Muslims. Each one of these aspects deserves its own lengthy elaboration. We only wish to stress two points. One is that the appearance of several nominations from the Central Asian Republics of the Soviet Union (one of these nominations was short-listed for Technical Review) allows the Award to consider itself now as the only cultural organism which truly reflects all the sub-cultures of the Muslim world. This is a welcome event indeed with considerable long-range importance for the Award. The second point is that the proper evaluation of some of the new schemes and projects for housing upgrading requires longer use than that needed to evaluate single buildings. As a result, we specifically recommend that the next Jury consider anew the East Wahdat scheme in Amman and the Incremental Development Scheme in Hyderabad. Both seemed to the Jury to have considerable merits which need a few more years to be properly appraised, since socially related architecture requires a flexible time frame for the determination of success or failure.

The Jury's decisions reward several of the directions visible in today's architecture in the Muslim world. These decisions should not be seen as an endorsement of all the implications of the projects involved, nor do they imply the rejection of values expressed in projects which were not premiated. Two examples illustrate our point. We discussed at great length the issue of revivalism as a fully thought-out recasting of forms created and used in the past or in vernacular traditions. The premiated projects include only some examples of that particular point of view, and it behoves the Award to acknowledge additional searches for a genuine, intelligent and tasteful revivalism whose mechanisms and values are not yet fully understood in an Islamic context. Thus, this Jury salutes the efforts of Nader Ardalan with Iranian architecture and of Sergo Sutyagin with Central Asian architecture who are or have been involved with an interpretation of formal values which should enlighten our understanding of the past and shape the forms of the future.

The second example of novelty lies in the efforts of individual patrons and of non-governmental organisations in premiated projects and in many that are not. We want to emphasise how much these efforts are a welcome component in the mosaic of contemporary architecture which, especially in its social aspect, was dominated by government or international bureaucracies. We are aware, of course, of the dangers of speculation and profiteering associated with some of these private activities, and this is why we add a note of caution to our satisfaction, but the new enthusiasm of the private sector for improving society is most heart-warming.

Finally, we wish to add that the message our decisions sends is not one of contradictions, but of simultaneous and parallel activities which identify some, certainly not all, of the aspirations and built forms of Muslim communities today.

These communities are in so many places and with so many hopes and ambitions that the solutions to their needs are bound to be different from each other. A jury's decision is a judgement of their quality, not necessarily of the ideologies they imply.

Jury Citations

Restoration of the Great Omari Mosque, Sidon, Lebanon

Partly destroyed and damaged by acts of war, the mosque of Sidon, originally a good example of the complex architectural history of the Lebanese coast, was successfully restored and rebuilt thanks to the generosity of a native son, the physical and emotional efforts of its users and the talents and competence of a team of architects and students from Beirut. The users refused to accept the building of a new mosque and preferred to rebuild their shattered world with a monument of their past. In doing so, they give a powerful example to all those places in the Muslim world and elsewhere which have been maimed by the horrors of war. In addition, the head of the restoration team rebuilt the mosque with scientific precision and with the taste and intelligence of one experienced in understanding the monuments of the past. This combination of human steadfastness in the face of tragedy, of restoration talent and inventiveness in particularly difficult circumstances, and of dedicated native patronage and sacrifice makes the reconstruction of the Great Omari Mosque a beacon in a tortured land and a sign of hope for the rebuilding of war-torn nations.

Rehabilitation of Asilah, Asilah, Morocco

In the area of rehabilitation, renovation and upgrading, the town of Asilah in Morocco stands out as an example of great success in the Muslim world. From a modest start but with ambitious vision, a few native sons of Asilah took it upon themselves to upgrade the physical and cultural environment of their town. With perseverance and skill, they managed to raise the consciousness of the people of Asilah and mobilise them to implement this vision. A small cultural festival was held in Asilah in the summer of 1978, attracting some one thousand visitors, mostly from nearby localities. This event, modest as it was, gave the people of Asilah self-confidence and pride, qualities which have grown steadily over the years. The Asilah Festival (the musim) now attracts some one hundred and twenty thousand visitors from all over the world; it has become the biggest cultural event in Morocco and one of the most important in the Arab world and Africa. This success is all the more remarkable as it relied exclusively on the participation of the town's inhabitants, including children and women, with no or minimal governmental or outside support. The men who initiated the process, and have since remained committed to it, attracted widespread attention in Morocco, Africa and the Arab world, with one of them becoming appointed as Minister of Culture in his own country.

Grameen Bank Housing Programme, various locations, Bangladesh

The Grameen Bank Housing Project attracted the Jury's attention from the beginning by the sensitivity and brilliance of its underlying concept. For here, in one of the poorest and most populous countries of the world, the compassion of Islam, the resilience of Bangladeshi rural Muslims, and the dedication of the personnel of the Grameen Bank, converge in a creative and skilful way to improve the lives of millions of people. The Grameen Bank, a cooperative non-governmental association, started a small credit programme to the rural poor, without collateral, for the purpose of initiating income-generating schemes. The initial success of this modest programme was indicated by a real rise in the income of the borrowers and by their reliability in paying back loans.

This encouraged the Grameen Bank to extend credit to its shelterless members – eighty-four per cent of whom are women – to build newer, modest but healthier houses, which are flood and water-resistant. The small housing loans average US $350 each and include the provision of four concrete columns, a pre-fabricated sanitary slab and twenty-six corrugated iron roofing sheets. The rest is left to each borrower to procure on an incremental basis. In the course of five years, hundreds of thousands of landless rural Bangladeshis benefited from the Grameen housing project, resulting in some 44,500 simple, healthier, diverse but equally beautiful houses. More important in this respect is the socio-economic process which has accompanied this housing loan programme. Men, women and children have been involved in both income-generating activities and house-building. Health conditions and education have improved immensely. The beneficiaries of the programme have paid back their loans, including five per cent interest, at a rate of ninty-eight per cent. What started as a housing-loan scheme has turned into an overall integrated development process. The previously marginal homeless poor in Bangladesh, especially women, are now socially empowered. The brilliant success of the Grameen Bank project has attracted the attention of serious development planners throughout the world: in 1985, the American state of Arkansas asked the Grameen Bank to send a mission to help plan a similar programme to upgrade the living conditions of its rural poor. The lesson of this success lies in the thoughtful concept and the participatory process behind it – which could be emulated, not imitated, throughout the Muslim and Third Worlds.

Citra Niaga Urban Development, Samarinda, East Kalimantan, Indonesia

Through perseverance, dedication and a total commitment to their task, the project's participants have convincingly demonstrated the viability and feasibility of participatory planning at both design and implementation levels. The result is development with equity where the benefits have been shared by all parties in the process: the street peddlers (*kaki lima*), the shop-keepers and the local government. Not only has the project achieved its social and economic objectives, it has also created a vibrant, well-designed and well-integrated urban centre which has become the pride of the town. In 1989, Samarinda was awarded the coveted Adipura Award by the Indonesian President as one of a group of cities which have successfully developed themselves. This is all the more remarkable as these results have been achieved through private and community involvement, without financial or technical assistance from the government or foreign donors.

The whole process has been a democratic one, culminating in the establishment of a management board representing the interests of the *kaki lima* through a cooperative, the shop-keepers, the local government and the consultants. This institutionalisation of the process guarantees continuity and maintenance for the project.

The concept is generic in nature and is being replicated in other cities, including the capital, Jakarta. It may enhance social effectiveness in facing increasingly complex situations in the future, where commercial interests must be harnessed in the process of urban development in more equitable ways. It can also be conceived as a social learning process, in which local governments increasingly encourage active public participation in a democratic process, preparing urban communities to face the imperatives of social transformation and modernisation.

Gürel Family Summer Residence, Çanakkale, Turkey

Through a sensitive, intelligent and unpretentious approach, this summer residence constitutes an architectural dialogue where landscape and building are of equal importance. The functions of living have been divided into component parts, each of which is self-contained, and both house and garden are positioned with careful thought, on a beautiful site overlooking the Aegean seashore.

These principles of juxtaposing spaces, economy of means, and simplicity of local construction can be a model for a range of uses and a variety of places. This residence is indeed a work of art in which nature and humanism occupy the first place.

Hayy Assafarat and the Al-Kindi Plaza, Riyadh, Saudi Arabia

The landscaping of the Hayy Assafarat and the Al-Kindi Plaza, which is part of it, were made possible by an enlightened client, the Riyadh Development Authority. The client requested high technological quality as well as an understanding of the local environment and heritage and his relationship to the architects and planners who worked on the project was exemplary.

The landscaping represents a realistic and imaginative understanding of the natural and spatial organisation in hot and arid regions. It takes into consideration the site's natural conditions and enriches them with new elements to create attractive sites and provide them with climatic protection and social privacy through artificial sand and stone hills. After considerable and sophisticated research and an accurate analysis of different types of local plants and trees which grow in the region and which do not need regular irrigation, a radically new and yet totally genuine environment was created for a self-sustained ecological system in the extensive landscape areas and even rich gardens. This unique environment has attracted Saudi and Arab families in Riyadh on Fridays and holidays and they have become recreational areas for social gathering providing the privacy required of traditional Islam. Finally, this scheme played a major role in convincing the governmental and public sectors to change their concepts on landscape, to align them with the local environment, and thus to benefit from natural strengths.

The Al-Kindi Plaza is part of the main public spine which forms an essential part of the Diplomatic Quarter. It contains a Public Square (maidan) near to the central mosque of the Diplomatic Quarter. These complexes can be considered as ideal models for cities in Islamic and Arab societies. They have attractively preserved the traditional link between the mosque and the other public services of the city. The success of the whole is demonstrated by the lively public events which take place on the Square on Fridays. It is the sensitivity to the environment on such a grand scale which distinguishes this project designed and implemented by a local firm from Riyadh.

Sidi el-Aloui Primary School, Tunis, Tunisia

The Sidi el-Aloui Primary School is premiated for its courageous exploration of traditional architectural forms as an elegant – and economical – response to contemporary educational needs. The design of this school, developed by a citizens' group as an alternative to standard governmental-type designs, represents a prototype of considerable value to developing societies. Utilising an area left open by an earlier project, it develops a unique relationship to the surrounding urban setting and especially to a public park adjacent to it. It has become not simply a school but also a place for community activities.

The concise and orderly pattern of its classrooms generates a simple volume, discreetly enhanced by the judicious use of ornament and handicraft. Harmonising unobtrusively with the old buildings and narrow streets of the medina, this school constitutes a remarkably urbane and responsible building-block in the overall fabric of the city.

Corniche Mosque, Jeddah, Saudi Arabia

It is the architect's skill in combining historically derived forms that is the main basis for the Jury's decision. Siting and technology distinguish this building from the great majority of mosques built today. The Corniche Mosque is one of three set as pavilions along the corniche of Jeddah, an unconventional but visually arresting arrangement that lends spiritual strength to the entire territory and proclaims to the outside world the presence of Islam. Technologically, the mosque is built according to methods that the architect has developed through research into the ways used in the construction of mostly Egyptian mosques in a traditional high culture of Islam. These beacons on the coast have also become conspicuous places of piety and rest for the population of this city. The architect should be cited as a proponent for innovative siting, for rethinking classical methods of building, and for the effort to compose formal elements in ways that bespeak the present and at the same time reflect the luminous past of Islamic societies.

Ministry of Foreign Affairs, Riyadh, Saudi Arabia

This project was noted for its intelligent use and interpretation of traditional architecture and of general Islamic urban concepts. The influence of vernacular architecture in it is abstract and at the same time fundamental. It is a contemporary work of architecture in harmony with the international architectural main-stream. The building mass is isolated from its surroundings and designed like a citadel, as the function and nature of this Ministry dictate such segregation for reasons of security and privacy.

In opposition to the blank and forbidding exterior, the interior spaces are volumetrically lively, exciting, spectacular and hierarchically organised around 'streets'. The extensive use of water and natural light softens and enhances the quality of interior spaces, in spite of less than successful decorative schemes. Simplicity and complexity are outstanding features of the design. This lavish and expensive building conveys a sense of economy and clarity.

National Assembly Building, Sher-e-Bangla Nagar, Dhaka, Bangladesh

> '. . . the most beautiful architecture in one of the poorest countries of the world. We are so proud.'

This idea has been voiced over and over by ordinary citizens, government officials and professional architects alike in Bangladesh. Faced with an imposing architectural work of extraordinary power, clarity of form and beauty, the jury could not help but question the compatibility of Sher-e-Bangla Nagar with the needs and aspirations of a poor country. Yet, review of the history of the building's design and construction, plus on-site studies, surveys, and discussions with people from many different groups in society, reveal that over time it has come to enjoy overwhelming approval, that it stands as a symbol of democracy in Bangladesh, and has influenced that country in a variety of beneficial ways. The architectural potency of this building derives in part from the clarity of its overall composition and from its scale, both conveying the centrality and importance of the activity of assembly that lies at the heart of a democratic and participatory structure of governance. Reaching beyond the architecture of the immediate area, the building has assimilated important archetypes of the region, among other ways through the extension of its park and water pools. But, it has also drawn upon architectural ideas of lasting value from many civilisations around the world. Through his thoughtful and intelligent search for form, the architect has clarified an approach to architectural design that does not copy elements of regional architecture, and that does not import either contemporary or historically derived vocabularies of form from other parts of the world. The architect has re-interpreted and transformed these ideas through a process that applied concepts of construction technology to conditions specific to the Dhaka locale. The result is a building that, while universal in its sources of forms, aesthetics and technologies, could be in no other place.

Institut du Monde Arabe, Paris, France

Blending harmoniously with the banks of the Seine and provided with a beautiful site in Paris, the Institut du Monde Arabe is a showcase of contemporary architecture which has become a popular attraction in Paris and a source of pride among the communities of Arabs and other Muslims. It aspires in its architecture to serve as a place of thought about Islamic culture and admiration for its artistic heritage and, alone outside of the Muslim world, it has given importance to contemporary arts from Arab lands. Although not successful in all aspects of its design and at times overly complex to use with ease and comfort, the geometry of its facades and the numerous activities it houses have succeeded in maintaining cultural exchanges between the Arab world and France; the initiators of the project, both French and Arab, have made a successful bridge between their cultures.

RESTORATION OF THE GREAT OMARI MOSQUE

SIDON, LEBANON

Client: The Department of Islamic Awqaf, Sidon. Architect: Saleh Lamei Mostafa, Cairo, Egypt. Patron: Rafiq al-Hariri, Paris. Completion date: January 1986.

The Great or al-Omari Mosque is located in the old city of Sidon which is situated about forty-five kilometres south of Beirut. This port city has a significant and ancient history which goes back to the second millennium BC. It suffered numerous destructions at the hands of the Assyrians, Persians, Greeks and Romans. Islam was introduced to Sidon in 636-37. The Crusaders took the city in 1100, but the politics of the region see-sawed, and it continued to change hands between Crusaders and Muslims until 1260 when it was badly destroyed by the Mongols. In 1291 the Bahri Mamluks from Egypt, under the Sultan Nasir Mohammed bin Qala'un, invaded and took the city. It remained under Mamluk influence until the arrival of Ottomans, whose rule lasted until World War I.

The mosque itself lies on a high mound to the west of the old city, overlooking the Mediterranean Sea. Results of the soil analysis on the part of the 'hill' which slopes towards the sea-front, and on which the western *riwaq* was built, showed that it was artificial. The most likely interpretation is that it once formed part of the ramparts of the Crusader fortress on which the mosque was later built. Only a few wall fragments remain of this Crusader fortress; these include parts of a buttress on the south facade, a few pointed arches, and the ribbed vault of the northern *riwaq* which still stand.

In the original refectory of this fortress a mosque was built, and named after Omar ibn al-Khattab. It is the oldest standing mosque in Sidon, and it was severely damaged by bombing and gunfire during the Israeli invasion of Lebanon in 1982. Its restoration was conceived and executed under the Israeli occupation, thus symbolising the political will and resistance of the local community who commissioned the work under such trying circumstances.

Natural and human catastrophes have caused many changes, and damaged the building. Sea storms in 1820, an earthquake in 1837, and the bombardment of the port by the British-Austrian fleet in 1840 have all taken their toll on the mosque. Modifications and repairs on the mosque in 1870 and 1895 respectively caused the reorientation of the window openings as well as the demolition of an earlier ablution fountain. Reconstruction of the vaults of the prayer room, the three domes of the southern *riwaq* and the east doorway to the courtyard were all undertaken during the 1895 repairs. Judging by its style, the minaret must belong to the building phase of 1848-49. The last restorations on the mosque were

One significant aspect of the restoration work was the repairing of cracks and repointing of the joints between the stones; OPPOSITE: The interior courtyard showing the high standard of workmanship evident in the masonry

carried out in 1979 when reinforced concrete roofs were built over the prayer hall and the western *riwaq*.

Many varied causes led to the deterioration of the Omari Mosque. Sea winds bearing salts and sand damaged the exterior face of the stones, especially those on the west facade. Changes in seasonal temperatures, especially diurnal extremes, resulted in the formation of fissures in the walls. A lack of funds meant that there was no proper maintenance of the building, cracks in the roof went unrepaired, and the ensuing seepage and leakage of water damaged the walls, masonry and plaster; furthermore fungi developed. The minaret suffered when its wrought-iron strengthening rings started to corrode. Leakages from the modern sewage system encouraged water infiltration. When the Awqaf finally got around to repairing the mosque in 1979 their use of reinforced cement only accelerated the deterioration of the building. It increased the load on the original structure, and weakened the fabric. Wherever the two materials met, the original and the new cement, the differences between their porosity, hardness and expansion rates caused further cracks to appear in the mosque.

The final straw was the 1982 bombing and shelling of the port of Sidon by the Israeli occupation forces. Since the Great Omari Mosque was the main centre of resistance against the Israelis, it became their focal shelling point from the sea. Extensive damage was caused, including the partial collapse of certain parts of the mosque, namely the vaulting of the prayer hall, its northern wall, and the southern *riwaq* with its three domes. The minaret became detached from the wall, longitudinal cracks appeared, and a number of stones were dislodged. The southern and western facades also developed numerous and deep cracks. Even the hill itself was scarred, pitted, and split by the impact of the shelling.

Following the destruction of the al-Omari Mosque, Mr Rafiq al-Hariri, a native of Sidon living and working in Saudi Arabia, offered to build the town a new mosque. The town decided otherwise; they preferred to rebuild and restore their old mosque. The preparation of the restoration project was entrusted to Prof Lamei Mostafa, and work commenced immediately after approval was granted by the Department of Antiquities and the Ministry of Awqaf in Sidon. The construction company, Oger Liban which was owned by Mr Hariri, provided the coordination. Photographs and measured drawings were made earlier by the architect and his students.

The aim of the restoration project was to prevent the collapse of the remaining and still standing parts of the mosque, to reconstruct the sections that had been destroyed and to consolidate the damaged areas. The mosque was to be restored to its former function as the Friday Mosque of Sidon where it could provide the local community with a gathering place for social, political and religious activities. Another objective was the revitalisation of the traditional building crafts of this economically depressed area of Southern Lebanon.

The Omari Mosque is the dominant architectural feature of the city. Situated in a densely populated part of the old town

with the sea-shore running along its west side, it has houses, a school and a bath-house bordering its north and east facades. The main access to the mosque is from the north through a lane which leads from the bath-house to the mosque. A second and more recent entrance can be found in the eastern *riwaq* which connects it with Zahr-al-Amir Street. The total ground floor area of the building comprises 1,500 square metres while the total site area is 1,975 square metres.

The plan of the mosque is a simple one; entrance is possible through the northern *riwaq* which in turn leads into an open courtyard that has *riwaqs* on all sides. Entry into the long, rectangular prayer hall is possible through the southern *riwaq* which has four cross vaults that spring from the walls, and which are supported by exterior buttresses. The other *riwaqs* have four cross-vaults over pointed arches that are supported by piers – only the central section of the southern *riwaq* is covered by three domes. The western *riwaq* is the deepest, and is covered by a pitched roof. The minaret is centrally positioned in the northern wall of the prayer hall.

The mosque is almost entirely constructed of local sandstone, quarried from Qasimiya near the southern border. The same mortar, a mix of lime and sand, was used throughout the original building. However, some of the later Ottoman work reveals the use of 'black pan mortar' made of lime, mud and ash, especially beneficial against humidity. Limestone is used only as an infill.

The principal concerns of the restoration project were the consolidation and reinforcement of the mosque to prevent its collapse. Investigations were conducted on the structural conditions of the building to determine the interventions that would be necessary. Analyses of the soils, mortar and stones had to be completed prior to the commencement of work. Documentation, drawings and photographs of the building fabric prior to restoration also had to be made. This was an essential task, needed both for the official records of the project as well as for distinguishing and differentiating the reconstructed and restored parts from that of the original.

All the elements that had been destroyed were rebuilt. These included walls, piers, arches, vaults, domes and the roof of the mosque. The upper, cylindrical section of the minaret was dismantled, the stones were brought down, numbered and restored to their original places. All small cracks were filled in. Concrete was removed from the vaulting and was replaced with a damp-proofing mortar. Salt accretions, fungi and dust were cleaned off the building. Later additions such as the mosaic tiles were replaced by a marble pavement which recreated the simple geometric designs already found in the prayer hall. New wooden doors and shutters, gypsum lattice windows with inlaid coloured glass (a prototype was made in Egypt and a reproduction was made on site), and metal lattices for the lower parts of the windows were specially manufactured for the mosque, as were the chandeliers and the lanterns. All of these were designed to be specifically appropriate for this historic setting. The wooden shutters were made of 'katrani' pine

The Mosque and minaret prior to restoration; OPPOSITE: A simple, rather than ornate minaret contrasts with a delicate wrought iron railing and wooden canopy to form a singular landmark in Sidon

collected from old buildings, and designed with motifs preserved on existing doors.

Finally, the hill on which the mosque stands was consolidated, its cracks and fissures were filled in with a mixture of lime, gypsum, ash and sand, and the foundations adjacent to the southern facade were strengthened. A reinforced concrete retaining wall was built to support and contain the soil.

During the restoration work any stones found on the site were re-used. When stones had to be replaced, stones from adjacent old buildings were found to take their place. Only a few of the larger elements such as lintels and drain spouts were made from new stone. They were traditionally worked with a hammer and chisel. New mortar was prepared, based on the analysis and mix of the original, using a mixture of lime, clay and ash. Kaolin was added for flexibility in places where expansion and contraction could occur due to temperature changes. Gravel was placed over the vaulting, and over an infill of lime, gypsum, ash and coarse sand.

Traditional techniques were employed wherever it was feasible to do so. This was especially true for the rebuilding of the collapsed domes, vaults and arches of the mosque. Traditional building crafts had to be relearned. As in other parts of the developing world, the introduction of cement and reinforced concrete had caused most of the old building techniques to be laid aside for the new. Even the craft for manufacturing the wooden shuttering for the domes and vaults had to be retaught; they were made and remade until the desired quality was attained.

The stones were cleaned with brushes and potable water. No chemicals or mechanical devices were used. Detailed recommendations were specified for the upkeep and maintenance of the building, including specific soaps for cleaning surfaces, and formalin which was to be used against fungi.

Only a few new materials were introduced into the restoration process. An epoxy resin mixed with sand was used to fill in the cracks and thereby consolidate the walls. It was also used to provide a damp-proof course. Another intrusive modern material was bars of steel, utilised for reinforcing. An iron anchor, covered with lead to avoid corrosion, was also introduced into the minaret in order to strengthen it.

An average of seventy-five workers constituted the work force. Druzes, Sunni Muslims and Christians, some brought from neighbouring mountain villages, worked together on this project. The Christians had to later leave Sidon.

The architects, and civil engineers, the contractor and the consultant were all local professionals. The architects were former students of Prof Saleh Lamei Mostafa (himself trained in architectural restoration at Aachen University in Germany), and the Great Mosque of Sidon was their first professional experience.

Work commenced in February 1983, but the actual restoration work began in July of that year. The project was completed by January 1986, and the Great Mosque was officially inaugurated on February 21st 1986.

FROM ABOVE: Bearing walls permit a regular pattern of stonework; rib vaults allow space for fenestration; OPPOSITE, FROM ABOVE: The restored prayer area, showing the intricate pattern of the wooden ceiling and brass lamps; the Mosque in context, on a high plateau overlooking the sea

The total cost of the restoration was seven million Lebanese Liras, or roughly about US $274,000. The cost proved to be higher than anticipated because of the high rate of inflation, and difficult working conditions under the Israeli occupation. Upon closer inspection (that is, once the scaffolding was erected), it was discovered that the building was in far worse structural condition than had been previously thought. The entire budget was donated by Mr Rafiq al-Hariri.

The Great Omari Mosque of Sidon was returned to its original function as the traditional symbol of the city. It now not only serves as a gathering place for all Muslims but it also houses all the political and social meetings of the town. Religious lectures and teachings are also part of its function. Students use it as a place to study their homework, benefiting from the free electricity and its quiet spaces.

Due to the political situation in Lebanon it has not been possible to make an on site survey of the mosque since it has received the Aga Khan Award. It is to be hoped that now the political situation has improved in Lebanon it will be possible for the outside world to visit this impressive monument. A special tribute must be paid to the people of Sidon, their sheer audacity in not being willing to give up on their mosque, reconstructing and restoring it even in the teeth of an alien occupying force. Their sense of enterprise is to be commended.

Floor plan; OPPOSITE: To overcome the difficulty of building on a steep slope, a massive stone terrace was built and this has been strengthened

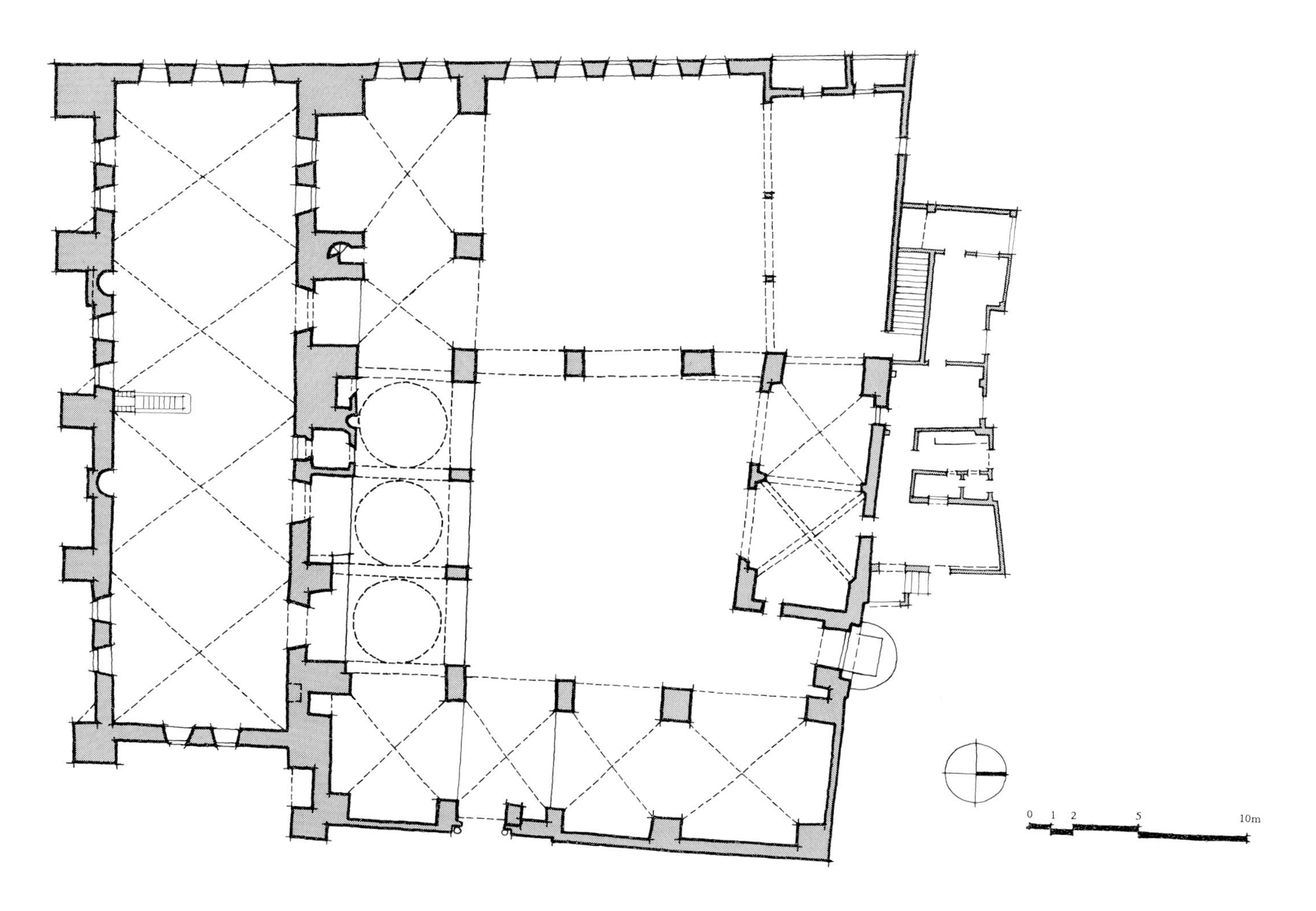

REHABILITATION OF ASILAH

ASILAH, MOROCCO

Client: Local Population and Municipality of Asilah. Patrons: Al-Moubit Cultural Association (Mohammed Benaïssa and Mohammed Melehi, founding members), Asilah. Completion date: 1978 and ongoing

The town of Asilah is strategically located on the shores of the Alantic Ocean, on the north-western tip of Morocco. It lies forty-two kilometres south-east of Tangiers in fairly flat countryside. It is an old town with walls and ramparts dating to the Portuguese occupation of Asilah, when it was used as a trading post. There is a natural harbour on the north-west side of the town. Inside the walls, the town follows the pattern of most old Arab medinas in the Mediterranean area, with courtyard houses lining the narrow alleyways. Some Spanish influence is evident on the facades of the houses especially in the style of the balconies.

The project began after the return of Mohammed Benaïssa to this, his home town, in 1968. He had been absent for twenty years. He bought a house in Asilah, renovated it, and began to live in it. The town, by all accounts, was a mess. It was filthy, the removal and disposal of the town's garbage was inadequate, and the streets were not paved. Asilah had no pharmacy or doctor, and the electricity lines and water mains were insufficient and out of date. Electric cables had been installed by the Spaniards in 1926.

To improve his town, Mohammed Benaïssa and his friend Mohammed Melehi, a painter and the President of the Moroccan Painters Association, decided to run for office. As soon as they were elected to the Municipal Council they initiated a study on the state of the town's cleanliness. They discovered that the eleven garbage collectors with their donkeys spent most of their time knocking on people's doors and asking people to give them their garbage. As there was no money in the Municipal coffers to change the system, they decided that the inhabitants of the town had to be involved, and made to participate in its improvement. Residents were asked to put their garbage outside their houses, ready for collection; this they did. It was from this humble beginning that the rehabilitation of Asilah started.

The next step was to improve the external appearance of the town. As both patrons of the project were involved in the world of art and culture they invited their artist friends to come and paint some walls in the town. In 1978 eleven painters accepted and participated in this exercise. Children helped, and they too were incorporated into maintaining the 'beauty' and the cleanliness of the town by competitions, prizes and gifts which were given to those who showed the most promise. Older people were also involved, and within a

FROM ABOVE: An interpretive site plan of Asilah utilising various dimensional techniques; aerial photograph of Asilah; OPPOSITE: Clean whitewashed surfaces now predominate in Asilah and make good environmental sense, helping interiors to keep cool; OVER-LEAF: Location plan; site plan of the medina; the crisp facades along main thoroughfares contrast with the rough grey stonework of the buildings still in the process of rehabilitation

0 10 20 50 100m

short space of time the whole population of the town was activated. The next move was to convince the Town Council to pave the streets, and rather than have the normal plain paving, Mohammed Melehi developed an artistic pattern of curved lines forming a series of waves. His reasoning was that the children of the town should have something beautiful to contemplate and walk on. These designs were adopted, and carried out.

With this successfully behind them, the two patrons decided that they should organise an annual summer art festival. It was named 'Asilah's Cultural Festival' and an association, The Al-Mouhit Cultural Association, was established to organise it. No sooner were these associations founded than they immediately clashed with investors who were interested in building tourist hotels and complexes and encouraging an 'International Festival' to bring the tourists to Asilah. Benaïssa strongly opposed this policy as intrusive and disruptive of the cultural integrity of Asilah. The conflict became a national one, and initiated a debate on the extent that a society should be willing to go to generate income from tourism. Benaïssa insisted all along that any project that did not include the local people's full participation, and which did not generate an income for them, would not benefit the town. Only the foreign investors and their local backers would benefit from such a project. The role of the local population would be relegated to that of photographers' models. Under combined pressure from the media and local population, the touristic hotel project failed to get a start.

Benaïssa transformed the festival into a *musim*, or season, thus relating it to religious and cultural activities of the town. The Spanish Government gave the Raissouni Palace to the project, and Benaïssa restored it for use as the festival's headquarters. Participants of the festival were also to be housed in the palace. In 1978 the first group of writers, thinkers and painters were invited for the inaugural summer of cultural activities in Asilah. The following year the King gave his blessing to the project, and officially asked the government agencies concerned to help Asilah. In 1983 Benaïssa became the President of the Municipal Council of Asilah, with Mohammed Melehi as his assistant.

The main objective of the project was the renovation and rehabilitation of the town of Asilah. This was to be funded by the cultural activities of the festival which were to be aimed at a Morrocan audience. The festival would also generate work and income for the local population. By providing the labour force or producing the materials, the people and the children of Asilah were made to actively participate in all aspects of their town's development. The project's hope for the future was that pride in their self-reliance would motivate the people of Asilah to become responsible for the upkeep, the general well-being, and future improvements of their town.

The improvement and extension of infrastructure including running water, sewerage and electricity was one of the many functional requirements of the new town, as was the restoration and rehabilitation of historical buildings such as the

New elements in the design have been carefully integrated into the existing fabric; OPPOSITE, FROM ABOVE: New housing has supplemented existing stock; gates and thresholds, for privacy, are an important part of the overall concept used in the town plan; OVERLEAF, FROM ABOVE: Asilah presents a unified and impressive aspect to the sea; an important feature of the Asilah rehabilitation scheme is the integration of existing and new buildings in an unobtrusive way

Portuguese fortifications, the Kamra Tower and the Raissouni Palace (early twentieth century). The construction of new houses within the old city were to replace those beyond salvation, while the public spaces were to be re-arranged for commercial activities, such as a market place. A new port was to be created and decorative pavings and murals designed by local artists were to be introduced.

The rehabilitation programme also included the transformation of the Raissouni Palace to accommodate art studios, workshops for children, laboratories and a hall for cultural gatherings; the building of the Hassan II exhibition centre and the creation of an open-air theatre within the old Portuguese walls, a hall for film shows, and an exhibition space for the plastic arts.

The campaign began by calling on all professional, educated people, and their relatives who had property in Asilah to renovate it, keeping within the traditional methods and modes. This call was answered with great enthusiasm by the local house owners as well as by Moroccan intellectuals and artists from elsewhere. Even expatriate Moroccans came flocking to Asilah to buy, and to renovate. As a result construction in Asilah has almost doubled during the last decade, already resulting, according to Benaïssa, in the renovation of about sixty per cent of Asilah's buildings. Official town records show that ten to fifteen dwellings are renovated each year, and this in a town that only comprises twelve hundred houses within its old walls.

Asilah's growth has been very tightly controlled. No hotel complexes or resort areas are allowed; the town prefers and wants to re-use the existing physical environment by restoring and upgrading it. Since 1981 the Al-Mouhit Cultural Association has annually renovated the sanitary facilities of ten houses belonging to poor people. Each house costs MDH 940 (US $1 = MDH 8.24) to improve. In summer the owners can rent out their houses to visitors or tourists for about MDH 2-3,000 per month while they stay with relatives.

New houses in Asilah are now built of reinforced concrete columns and beams although some use load-bearing brick walls and partitions. There are also load-bearing stone walls. Reinforced, hollow tiles are used for the floors of new buildings. Concrete and hollow bricks are the most common materials used for walls, while the facades are generally rendered with cement covered with a lime wash. The finishing can include cedar woodwork, as well as traditional ceramic tiles (*zelij*). Marble and other expensive materials are rare. These new houses are built in plots left empty after the demolition of the original old houses. They frequently integrate elements salvaged from the ruins – doorways, window frames and arches are the most popular elements collected.

Most of the renovation and restoration work has been carried out by local master masons and workers using traditional construction methods and materials. The technology is fairly simple as the town does not possess skilled labourers.

Traditional, casual souks, which have sprung up along interstitial spaces between walls and groups of housing, provide a colourful contrast to the solidity of vertical surfaces; OPPOSITE, FROM ABOVE: Masonry lookouts punctuate the long sea-wall; small details, such as stepped cornice crenellations and repeating arcades, provide a sense of unity throughout the town

The project started in 1978 and is ongoing; the total cost is therefore unknown. However, the town's budget increased from MDH 1,800,000 before 1978 to 10,900,000 in 1989. This gives some idea of the costs since the increase includes all the maintenance costs of the town plus the salaries of the employees. The town is continuously looking for external money to help with the restoration process. For example, the Portuguese Government financed some of the renovation work on the old town, and Shell Oil company gave the town two hundred garbage barrels.

The whole town of Asilah has benefited from its rehabilitation. In 1982 the population of the town was eighteen thousand; today it may be as high as twenty-five thousand, out of which only four to five thousand inhabit the old town. The average income per family was less than US $50 a month in the 1970s; today it is approximately US $140. Most of the town's people are quite proud of Asilah, and of the fact that during the last decade it has become well known to all of Morocco and even internationally, especially after winning the Aga Khan Award. They are pleased and feel lucky that they have better water, electricity, and sewage systems than before, and a telephone network that works. On the other hand they feel intimidated by the summer cultural activities, and say they are too sophisticated for them, 'above their level' in the words of a local inhabitant. Other complaints range from the costly price of the festival tickets, to dislike of the wave patterns of the murals, or even to the un-Islamic aspects of some of the cultural events, and the loss of their beaches through the building of a new port. These first charges are refuted by the Town Council who say that they distribute six hundred (out of two thousand) tickets free of charge to those who really cannot afford to buy them.

The most serious charge against the project seems to be that presented by many of the poorer residents of the old town who say that they have been forced to move out because of the high costs of upkeep demanded of them for their old houses. The land value was five MDH per square metre prior to the creation of the summer festival, and no one was buying. Now the land values have risen sharply and people are benefiting by selling their houses, or selling small plots within their property to help restore the rest. Benaïssa defends the ideas and policies of the Association by saying 'we changed the people's income without changing their behaviour, preserving the origin of the soul while developing the appearance'. He also states that Al-Mouhit gives financial aid to help those who cannot afford the renovation of their property. However, typically, and as in other developing countries, the people of Asilah, especially the young, do not want to dirty their hands. They want to have an office job or work in a leather factory, emulating what they think is the bourgeois European thing to do. They do not want to accept manual jobs.

Each summer Asilah is inundated with thousands of tourists and visitors, 150,000 of them. They stay in the hotels and rent the houses, they eat in the restaurants, and boost the

Aside from the high visibility of minarets, relatively constant cornice heights contribute to an overall impression of continuity throughout the urban area; OPPOSITE: The minaret of the Friday Mosque is a prominent vertical landmark, that helps visitors establish a directional reference in the compact context of Asilah

commercial activities by buying the local crafts. A multitude of services are generated by this yearly invasion, of which the local people are the chief beneficiaries. During these summer months they accumulate the resources that help them to survive for the rest of the year when the economy is moribund, and the people fall back on their old ways. For a few months each year the town, its municipality and people are dragged out of their lethargy by the remarkable vision of Benaïssa, Melehi and their friends.

By providing the infrastructure, a sound economic basis, the necessary know-how, and the professional knowledge and good sense of its members, the Al-Mouhit Cultural Association hopes to keep on helping and educating the people, especially the youth of the town. Today, the town is clean, its streets are paved and electricity and telephones work. Even though the problem with the sewage has not been completely resolved, the plans for upgrading it are there.

However, danger is still present in the shape of the speculators and builders who keep up the pressure on the people to sell. They want to take advantage of the unique situation of the town to build new houses, to change and modernise the town, in fact to urbanise it. That, of course, would destroy Asilah. It is, therefore, of the utmost importance that an urban rehabilitation plan for Asilah be made by a specialised team. This plan would then have to be accepted by all parties concerned, including the town and the Ministry of Awqaf, and then placed under the jurisdiction of the Ministry of Interior. Without an official policy the town of Asilah could easily lapse into the same nightmarish scenario that has afflicted and destroyed so many scenic spots on the Mediterranean. Tourism can bring great economic benefits to an area. It can also just as easily destroy, killing the goose that lays the golden egg. It has to be carefully regulated and controlled.

The horseshoe arch, which is identified with the Magreb, is echoed throughout public and private spaces; OPPOSITE, FROM ABOVE: The combination of a hot, dry climate most of the year, and proximity to the ocean means that there are frequently spectacular sunsets at Asilah, with pinkish-red hues transforming the relative severity of white walls

GRAMEEN BANK HOUSING PROGRAMME

VARIOUS LOCATIONS, BANGLADESH

Client: Landless Members of Grameen Bank. Planner: Grameen Bank (Mohammed Yunus, Managing Director), Dhaka. Completion Date: 1984 and ongoing

Bangladesh is a tropical country with seasonal monsoons during which a high rainfall occurs. Associated with the monsoons are tidal surges and an increased run-off from the mountains to the north of the country; these can, and do, cause disastrous floods. Cyclonic storms are also frequent in the south. It is a poor and populous land of seventy-eight million inhabitants, eighty-five per cent of whom can be considered rural. Of those, sixty per cent can be classified as landless. In a country where the national income per capita is estimated at about US $140 per annum, the income level of the landless rural population is virtually that of the destitute. It is this landless rural population that are hit the hardest by the annual monsoon flooding and the cyclones. Their sufferings are augmented by the fact that they usually have to live on marginal lands, in frail, feeble shelters or makeshift homes that leave them exposed to every risk.

Although the landless poor provide the bulk of the agricultural labour force in Bangladesh, a substantial proportion of them also engage in a variety of other activities such as weaving, mat making, small scale trading, rearing goats or sheep, keeping pigeons, sewing, rice husking and making pottery. Because they lack the financial resources their time is not used productively, they cannot buy the materials or tools that are needed to allow them to expand and rise above the poverty line.

The Grameen Bank Programme was started in 1976 in the village of Jobra by Dr Mohammed Yunus, the then Director of the Rural Economics Programme, of the Department of Economics in Chittagong University. It set out to provide credit to the rural, landless poor for income generating activities, and offered it to them at the low interest rate of sixteen per cent. Because they lack the collateral, the poor are normally barred from obtaining credit from official institutions. They are then forced to borrow from the private sector at exorbitant interest rates.

The significant and truly revolutionary aspect of the Grameen Bank Programme was that it required no collateral from its poor customers. They had to repay their debt through their own commercial or artisanal activities. The condition of the Grameen Bank Programme was that people organise themselves into small groups who could act in concert and with discipline. The group would oversee the punctual payments of the loan instalments of all their

A participant in the programme proudly displays the payment book which made her house possible; OPPOSITE: A clean raised concrete slab, on which to build, has an enormous impact on hygiene, self-worth and human dignity

members – if not the group had to pay. This ensured sufficient peer pressure from within.

The Grameen Bank Programme was transformed into an independent bank with the name of the Grameen Bank in 1983. The Government provided sixty per cent of the initial paid up share capital while forty per cent was held by the borrowers of the Bank. Recently this was revised and set at twenty-five per cent for the Government, with the remaining seventy-five per cent to belong to the borrowers. The Bank's conditions for membership are as follows: any person whose family owns less than 0.5 acres of cultivable land, and whose assets together do not exceed the market value of one acre of medium quality land in the area, is eligible for loans for income-generating activities from the Grameen Bank. Only one person from each household is allowed to become a member. To get a loan he or she must form a group of five like-minded people from similar economic and social backgrounds. They elect a chairman and secretary, and hold weekly meetings. Sometimes several groups in a village get together and form a 'centre' with an elected Centre Chief and Deputy Chief. The Centre Chief then conducts the weekly meetings, and is responsible for the observance of the rules of the Bank. Between two and ten groups can form a centre, the average being six groups. Eighty-four per cent of the Grameen Bank members are women. In fact, the belief of the Bank is that women are a potential and reliable economic force amongst the poor. Over the past decade the members of the Bank have evolved a manifesto, called the 'Sixteen Decisions', which is adhered to by all the groups.

Loans are given to individual members or to the group as a whole, each loan being valid for one year only. It is paid back in weekly instalments, each being two per cent of the total amount. In addition, every group member deposits one taka per week (TK 30 = US $1) as a personal saving which is placed into the Group Fund Account. When a group member receives a loan an obligatory deduction of five per cent of the loan amount, known as a 'Group Tax', is deposited into the Group Fund Account where it can be used for the benefit of the members. On approval from the group, members can then borrow from this fund. In addition, a member pays a weekly sum into an 'Emergency Fund' which is set at a rate of one-fourth of the total interest being paid to the Bank. This is basically an insurance against default, death, disability, accident or other disasters. The maximum individual loan is TK 5000 (US $166), although proven borrowers can get more. The smallest loan on record was for one taka.

Each centre is looked after by a Grameen Bank Branch Assistant who attends the weekly meetings and collects the payments. He identifies future customers, distributes the loans, supervises the groups under his charge, and ensures that accounts are kept and payments paid back on time. In fact, he is involved in many extension activities with his groups. Each Grameen Bank Branch Assistant is responsible for up to ten centres, and, with an average of six groups per centre, that means seeing up to three-hundred people per

Women have played a key role in the success of the lending programme, and have also been directly involved in house construction; OPPOSITE: A light inexpensive rush skin, wrapped around the bamboo

week. He works out of a branch office that supervises and services some sixty centres located in about twenty villages. Ten branch offices are supervised by one Area Office covering an area of two hundred square miles which in turn is supervised by a Zonal Office. Each Zonal Office looks after an average of eight Area Offices. These Zonal Offices have a high degree of autonomy and are given a free hand to administer their areas. The head office is based in Dhaka, and it oversees the whole project.

By March 1989 the Grameen Bank had 53,5170 members spread out over 11,793 villages in nine zones of Bangladesh. There are 571 branches in operation looking after 21,612 centres. Of these centres, 18,831 are comprised of female groups and only 2,781 are of male groups. Excluding the Housing Loans, the Grameen Bank has currently distributed just over TK 4,013,536,000, or US $133,764,533. As of June 1988 the astonishing recovery rate was 98.35 per cent.

The Housing Loan Programme was initiated in October 1984 after a National Workshop during which Grameen Bank workers exchanged their practical experiences and ideas. From this exchange it became clear that as the income generating capacity of the Grameen Bank borrowers improved their demand for better housing increased. The decision was then made to start a Housing Loan Programme as a specific and important part of the Grameen Bank operations, and not just as an adjunct to another loan. Its aim was to make funds available for Grameen Bank members of good standing for building new houses, or rehabilitating their old ones. Only members who regularly paid their dues on time, and who adhered to the rules, were considered for these loans. And because the sums involved were much larger than those that were available through the general loan programme, new lending policies and procedures had to be set up. Preference, as always, was given to the most needy.

A two tier system was established. The larger loan, for amounts up to TK 18,000, was called the 'Standard Housing Loan', while the smaller loans, of up to TK 10,000, were called 'Basic Housing Loans'. They were to be repaid at a rate of TK 1,000 per year, so that a person taking out a loan of TK 15,000 had up to fifteen years to pay it back. The housing loan is charged at five per cent interest instead of the sixteen per cent interest charged for the regular or short term loans.

The Grameen Bank Housing Loan Programme covers a wide geographical zone which includes a range of architectural styles. Most of the houses occupied by the poor are of single storeys with one or two rooms at the most, and with the cooking area and animal shelter clustered around the house forming a yard or outdoor work area. The house space is multi-purpose and acts as a sleeping area, and a storage space for all the utensils that the family owns including those for income generating activities such as weaving and sewing. A ceiling level platform, built using the base of the roof truss, frequently acts as the repository for valuable objects. A number of the houses have interior altars.

FROM ABOVE: Structural system of basic units; quickly drying mud allows for creative variation and different organic forms in each structure; concrete posts for the houses have been pre-fabricated, but in a far less energy-intensive way, showing the possibilities of appropriate technology; OPPOSITE: Once a basic structural frame is provided, individual owners are able to erect readily available reed panels to enclose their houses; OVERLEAF: Deep roof overhangs accommodate the small cottage industries, such as weaving, which have helped residents improve their standard of living and repay the bank loan

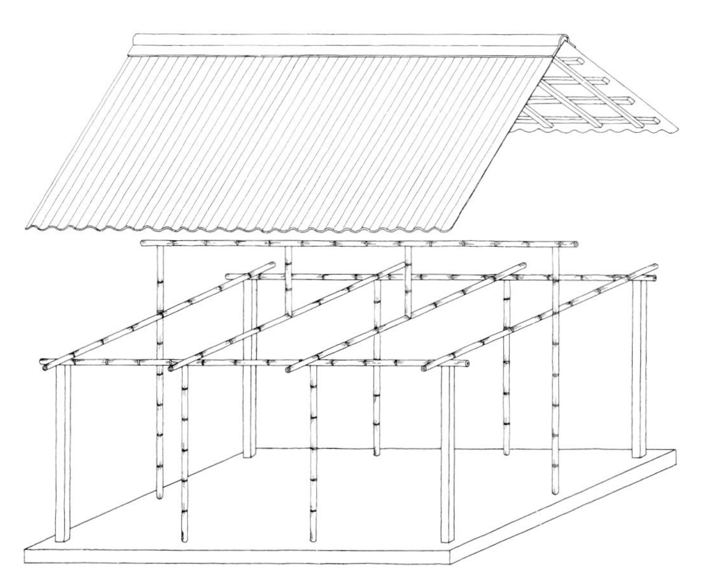

The archetypal house form consists of a rectangular building with a pitched roof, and hipped or gable ends. They are small, and can measure from 2 x 3 metres to 4 x 7 metres in size. Most pre-Grameen Bank houses seem to have been smaller than those built with the loans. All are built on raised earth platforms to preserve them from the rising flood waters of the rainy season. Some houses have windows, others do not. Doorways, made of bamboo matting or wood, seem to provide most of the interior light and usually open inwards.

In the central area of Bangladesh the houses are mostly built with a bamboo or wood frame that can support a lightweight wall made of either bamboo matting or jute sticks. The facades are frequently plastered with mud. Thatched roofs are made of grass, rice stems, bamboo matting or jute sticks. All these materials are not durable, and have to be replaced almost every two years. Yearly flooding adds to their brief lives. So thatched roofs are dispensed with as soon as the owner can afford to buy corrugated sheeting. Sometimes even the walls are replaced with sheeting.

Bamboo and jute sticks are the cheapest materials to build with. They are also light and can be removed and carried to a new location at flood time, and/or easily replaced.

Bamboo is now in short supply and sometimes has to be imported from India, thus increasing its price, but jute is still the cheapest material. However, it does not last as long as bamboo and is easily attacked by termites. The floors are usually of mud, and frequent mud coats gives the houses a neat and clean look. North of Dhaka where flooding is common the houses have massive rammed earth and cob walls, but in 1988 the flood waters rose so high that many of these houses collapsed. People now prefer to build a frame house with light walls, or else include columns in the corners to help support the roof. More expensive materials, such as fired brick and reinforced concrete, are rarely used as building materials by the poor.

The Grameen Bank Housing Programme proposes a basic house which can be built with a Basic House Loan, and which can be modified and extended by the borrowers if their resources permit it. A Standard House Loan would, of course, provide a larger house but the materials remain the same. The basic house has a usable floor area of at least twenty square metres. Four reinforced concrete columns, manufactured by the Grameen Bank, are supplied to each borrower. The early Grameen Bank Housing Loan houses had wooden posts but these proved to be susceptible to termites and unstable during the floods. A more secure structure was needed.

Reinforced columns were introduced and have proven to be very successful. They provide a secure attachment point for the walls, and they hold up the roof in such a stable manner that in times of floods the people can safely sit on them. The columns are sunk upright into the ground at the four corners of the house, to a depth of 0.50 metres.

Additional posts, made of wood, bamboo or reinforced concrete have to be provided by the borrower, and depend on the resources to hand. The loan allows for the obligatory purchase on the local open market of eighteen corrugated iron sheets, measuring 2.438 x 0.820 metres each, and sufficient to cover the basic house with a simple pitched roof. This can be supported by a wooden or bamboo roof frame which, in turn, is supported by the four columns and any other secondary posts.

Walls can be filled in with any material chosen and bought by the borrower who also decides on the number and types of windows and doors he or she requires. Grameen Bank staff favour doors and shutters that open inwards because they are not exposed to the sun and rain, and can therefore survive longer. Heights of plinths and floors are left up to the borrowers. The Grameen Bank has a plan for the basic house, and makes sure that at least the minimum requirement is achieved. However, the borrower is basically responsible for the real design of their house. And even though they usually choose materials that belong within the local architectural style for their roofs and as fillers, no two houses ever seem the same.

Since mid-1988, the programme has also required the borrower to build a latrine for the house, using a latrine's base with syphon and cement liners for the pit. These are manufactured by the Grameen Bank production yards, and are given with the rest of the materials at the start of the house, but the Grameen Bank does not advise on their placement. The Grameen Bank does not involve itself with such details as the siting of a house, its orientation, or its relation to nearby buildings. They also do not provide loans for public facilities; however, some centres are using their savings fund for setting up schools for the younger children.

The reinforced concrete pillars and the latrine kits are manufactured at thirty-four different sites across the country, using moulds which are easily transportable according to demands. The local branch office only needs to specify the amounts required. The masons running the production units receive a loan from the Grameen Bank at sixteen per cent interest to help them finance the work. The borrower has to arrange the transport. Two pillars can be moved in one rickshaw van, and/or three men can carry one pillar at a time. Each column is 3.35 metres long and 13.3 centimetres squared in cross section. The production of these pillars operates as an independent income generating unit. A mason and five labourers can produce twenty-nine columns per day; each sells for TK 325. They are made with a mix of two parts cement, to four parts sand, to two parts of brick chips. Each column also has four ten millimetre diameter bars and thirteen links. The person who takes out the loan pays the workers.

The concept and the design of the houses originated in Bangladesh. Many of the materials are local, although corrugated sheeting is essentially an imported product. Cement comes from local factories as well as from Indonesia, and the steel for reinforcing is milled in Bangladesh.

All the Grameen Bank Housing loans are given to the rural poor who either live in rural settlements, or on plots of land

sited by road embankments or fields. There is such a great variety in these houses that they cannot be described in general terms. The following descriptions of three specific loans will suffice as examples of houses built with housing loans granted by the Grameen Bank.

Afiya Begum has been a member of the bank for nine years. She took out a house loan after her house was destroyed by floods. Her new house stands on a high platform, fourteen square metres, which rises several metres above the level of the paddy fields that surround it on three sides. The Dhaka-Tangail road lies alongside the fourth side. The house consists of a single room measuring 6 x 4 metres, and an outbuilding, 2 x 4 metres in size, that functions as a kitchen. The two sections are positioned at right angles to each other and so create a small open-air space that also acts as an outdoor cooking area. She is also intending to build an outside latrine on the site. Her husband and three children share the house. In this small space she keeps goats and ducks which help to augment her income. She bought the land from a local landowner with a loan from Grameen Bank.

Kamala Begum lives with her husband in a new Grameen Bank loan house, situated some fifty metres away from the Dhaka-Tangail road, in a small compound with three other households. Her husband owned the eight-hundred and fifty square metres on which they built their house, but since she was the Grameen Bank member the title deeds were transferred to her name. The houses have a large open area between them, and sit high above the level of the paddy fields around them. She earns her living by sewing, using a machine she bought with a loan from the Grameen Bank. From her savings she bought her husband a rickshaw.

Rahissa Begum has a two-room, 5 x 3 metre house which was built with a Grameen Bank housing loan in the village of Habibpur, Munshiganj Upazila District. The village consists of many clusters leaving little room for expansion. Her house faces the river bank on one side and a small neighbourhood open area on the other three. She has a kitchen shelter. Her husband owned the land and it was transferred to her name. Although it is difficult to expand she wants another loan to add an extension for her four sons and one daughter who live with them. Her income comes from two milk cows which she bought with Grameen Bank loans.

The Grameen Bank Housing Loan Programme started in October 1984 with a potential house loan of up to TK 15,000. In 1984 these came to a total of 317 loans. The number rose in 1985 to 1,264, but they decreased in 1986 when there were only 416 new housing loans given out. After the disastrous floods of 1987 there was a sharp increase in the number of borrowers, 21,366 in 1987 and 21,148 in 1988. This increase coincided with the two tier house loan system mentioned above. In 1988 these loan plans were modified and a new, Small Housing Loan was introduced for amounts up to TK 8,000 and renamed the 'Basic Housing Loan'; the sum was later raised to TK 10,000. The 'Moderate Housing Loan' was increased to TK 18,000. The Basic Loan is taken nine times

FROM ABOVE: The plaiting of rush siding, reinforced with bamboo strips is achieved with heavy gauge steel wire, which makes the wall surprisingly strong and durable; as with posts, sanitary units for each house are also prefabricated, which has helped in cutting costs; OPPOSITE, FROM ABOVE: Choice of material makes a significant difference in the appearance of each dwelling, but the cost of each is similar

more often than the Moderate. In all cases, it is not necessary to take the maximum amount.

The Basic House Loan of TK 10,000 which has to be repaid back at five per cent interest breaks down as follows:

Reinforced concrete pillars at TK 325 each	TK 1,300
Two bundles of corrugated iron sheets	TK 5,000
Sanitary latrine	TK 500
Other materials, roof frame etc	TK 3,200
Total	TK 10,000

By the end of 1988, the Grameen Bank had distributed TK 337,582,618 to 44,556 borrowers, at an average of TK 8,058 per head. Payments are made on a weekly basis at a minimum rate, but if the borrower wishes, the repayments can be larger and the time period shortened.

But the maximum period is fixed in the ratio of years to thousands, so TK 18,000 has to be repaid in eighteen years. The repayment rate is running close to a hundred per cent.

Funding for the project has primarily come from the Bangladesh Central Bank and from foreign donors, including NORAID, SIDA, CIDA, GTZ and IFAD.

The maintenance cost for these houses is very low. It basically includes the replacement, every two or three years, of the jute and bamboo matting on the walls. The reinforced concrete pillars should last for eighteen years maximum, although the corrugated iron sheeting will not survive that long. Termite attacks and humidity cause the deterioration of the organic materials used in the walls, and these have to be replaced at intervals. Some families have experimented and used the poison aldrin at the base of bamboo posts to try to limit the termite attacks; others have coated these posts with liquid bitumen.

Technically, these house loans are sound. The houses' protection from the rain is good, an important point in a monsoon country, and for most households it is a significant improvement on their traditional housing. They also withstand the floods better. After the 1988 floods the Grameen Bank house owners spent less money repairing their houses than those who had traditional houses.

This was also apparently true for the disastrous cyclones that hit the Bangladesh coastline in the spring of 1991. The Grameen Bank house owners fared much better, and they lost less of their belongings. The reinforced columns provide a strong frame for the house as long as soil erosion is not a major problem. If erosion becomes serious then the columns can be removed and transported to safer ground.

The level of technology required for building and maintaining these houses is perfectly adapted to the users. All the materials are familiar, and no new technical innovation is required. The users have faith in the materials used in their houses, all of which have been tried and proved successful. Innovative techniques and materials would probably not be popular with people of such modest needs.

The response to the programme has proved its success and greatness. The number of borrowers is increasing, and the Grameen Bank hopes to add another twenty-two million US dollars to their fund by 1992. Grameen Bank also plans to expand the areas it serves, but only after it has trained the necessary staff to carry out this work. The staff are dedicated to the objectives of the Bank. In fact, they are really the ones who are responsible for the success of the operation, and it could not have been achieved without their hard work.

The reaction of the users has been difficult to measure. The Bangladesh Institute of Development Studies has tried to assess the reaction of the Grameen Bank Housing Loan house occupiers. From a survey conducted in the Tangail, Dhaka and Rangpur Zones, on a sample of a hundred and sixteen cases, the benefits from moving into the new houses in the order of their importance is given as follows:

– things are saved from damage caused by rain
– things are saved from thieves
– a decreased intensity of diseases
– increase in the quality of work
– increase in social dignity
– capability of doing more as mental strength increases

The most significant factor seems to be that everyone that was visited had plans to go on adding to their houses. Many have already enlarged their original investments by adding better windows, cemented floors, a roofed verandah or even additional rooms. However, one cannot and should not disassociate the physical product of a house and the provision of a loan from the fact that Grameen Bank has been providing general loans for the promotion of finance generating activities among the Grameen Bank borrowers. The Housing Loan, and its end result, is an effective and successful operation because the borrowers are already engaged in activities stimulated by a general Grameen Bank loan which enables them to cope with the repayments on the house, and embellish it with savings made from their self-employment.

The two parallel aspects of the Grameen Bank loans are what makes it successful. It would not have been possible for poor people to take out a loan for a house without an income to repay the loan. The income generating loans provide them with the wherewithal to do that. The vision of Dr Mohammed Yunus in creating such a package is to be commended. It is truly an extraordinary project.

OPPOSITE, FROM ABOVE: Not all roofs are tin, as other choices have been allowed; the Grameen Bank Housing Programme has shown how minimal means can make an important difference in the lives of people who had previously held out little hope for a better life

Citra Mahakam

CITRA NIAGA URBAN DEVELOPMENT

SAMARINDA, INDONESIA

Client: Municipal Government, Samarinda. Developer: PT Pandurata Indah (Didik Soewandi, Director), Samarinda. Architects: Antonio Ismael, PT Triaco and PT Griyantara Architects, Jakarta. Sponsor: Institute for Development Studies (NGO), Jakarta. Users: Koperasi Pedagang Pasar (the informal sector cooperative), Samarinda. Completion Date: July 1986

Samarinda is situated on the banks of the Mahakam River, and is the provincial capital of East Kalimantan in Borneo. Borneo is one of the major timber centres of Indonesia, and Samarinda acts as the main depot for its region. In fact, the Dutch founded the town in the nineteenth century specifically for that reason, and timber logs were shipped down the river from its port. More than half the total timber of Indonesia is exported from the port of Samarinda. This assures the continued prosperity of the town even as it incurs a devastating effect on the forests. The other economic activity of the region is off-shore oil exploration. The logging, oil exploration and exploitation are mostly in the hands of Japanese, South Korean or Taiwanese companies. It is, therefore, a high employment area with a continuously growing population of the young and the poor, seeking work in these trades.

Samarinda has become a focal town for immigrants. The town did not have a housing stock that could accommodate this influx, so the immigrants set up shacks and squatter settlements, adding to the lacklustre and characterless look of the town. The tropical, humid climate, with its incessant and heavy rainfall (1,850 millimetres annually), water-logs the land and then erodes it, and makes it an unpleasant environment to live in. However, that does not seem to stop the flow of immigrants who come in from East and Central Java, South Sulawesi and South Kalimantan. Since they cannot all find official work they seek 'hidden employment' in the town, in retail facilities or as hawkers. These pavement hawkers or *kaki lima* have grown in number, from a thousand in 1983 to five-thousand by 1985. These are the registered figures; a more accurate number would probably be closer to six-thousand. This is reflected in the rise of the town population which rose from 137,918 in 1971 to 343,198 by 1987. In 1985 the Municipality of Samarinda began to consider special programmes to tackle the problems of the street hawkers who were choking the city's streets. Although *kampung*, or urban slum, improvement schemes had been going on since 1975, the Citra Niaga project was the first commercial, and non-housing rehabilitation programme undertaken by the city.

The story of the project is interesting. Mr Soewandi an ex-Governor of East Kalimantan was worried about the slum areas that sprawled across the centre of Samarinda. He asked his son, Didik, who had just returned from studying at Berkeley University, whether he could find a collaborator and

A theme of architectural variety, within an overall unified scheme, is evident throughout the Samarinda project; OPPOSITE, FROM ABOVE: As a village within a village, Citra Niaga has an identity of its own; tall towers with pyramidal roofs provide a distinctive identity for the project

BADAN PENGELOLA CITRA NIAGA
BADAN PENGELOLA CITRA NIAGA

develop a scheme for a town centre. Didik contacted his friend Antonio Ismael, a Berkeley architect who was working on a community project in Mexico. Together, they coopted the services of Adi Sasono from the Institute for Development Studies, an NGO that was already working in Samarinda. They prepared a scheme and took it up through the maze of the government bureaucracy, level after level, until it was finally presented to and approved by the Minister of Interior. The decree was promulgated on July 27, 1985.

The arguments used to put the ideas across to the Government officials were the following:
– Samarinda is the capital city of East Kalimantan and should show a modernised front for all sectors of the economy. New development activities need to be undertaken for that purpose;
– the people's participation, at all levels, would improve their apathetic attitude and should transform them into a more dynamic and active body;
– a start should be made in the worst slum areas of the city, and new commercial facilities should be established there as part of the town's transformation process.

The Government's approval, when it came, was subject to the conditions that State finances were not to be used, and that thirty per cent of the space at Citra Niaga would be allocated to street hawkers who would constitute sixty per cent of all the shop owners of the centre. The reason that approval was necessary from the Central Government was because the project required the use of land belonging to the Government for private development. Also the project was proposing to use new methods of urban management which were unacceptable to the local Municipality, or rather they could not act on them without prior approval from the higher authorities in Jakarta. The key to this type of management was the mobilisation of various key resources, not only the Local and Central Government and the private sector, but, most importantly, to include the active participation of the local inhabitants, the low income families who illegally occupied the area in question. The project design was not only to be a self-cost recovery/self-financed and self-sustaining enterprise but also to be a profitable venture, an altogether ambitious undertaking.

The Citra Niaga site is flat, and surrounded on all sides by commercial urban development and vehicular roads that are crowded with a wide variety of mobile transports. Buildings in the immediate neighbourhood are generally two storeys in height. Beyond the site itself, where the land prices are higher, the buildings are concrete structures, four and five storeys high. Immediately to the south is the Niaga-Seltan dual carriageway, created at the time of the project.

The designer was clear in the objectives of his scheme. They included:
– the creation of a place where the rich and poor could mutually exist;
– the accommodation of all economic levels of the population together and with no segregation;

A convenient, open shelter, which serves as a meeting point in the midst of the project; OPPOSITE: Carved wood ornithological figures and sloped roof forms add a traditional aspect to the high tower used as a landmark in the development; OVERLEAF, FROM ABOVE: Site plan; elevations

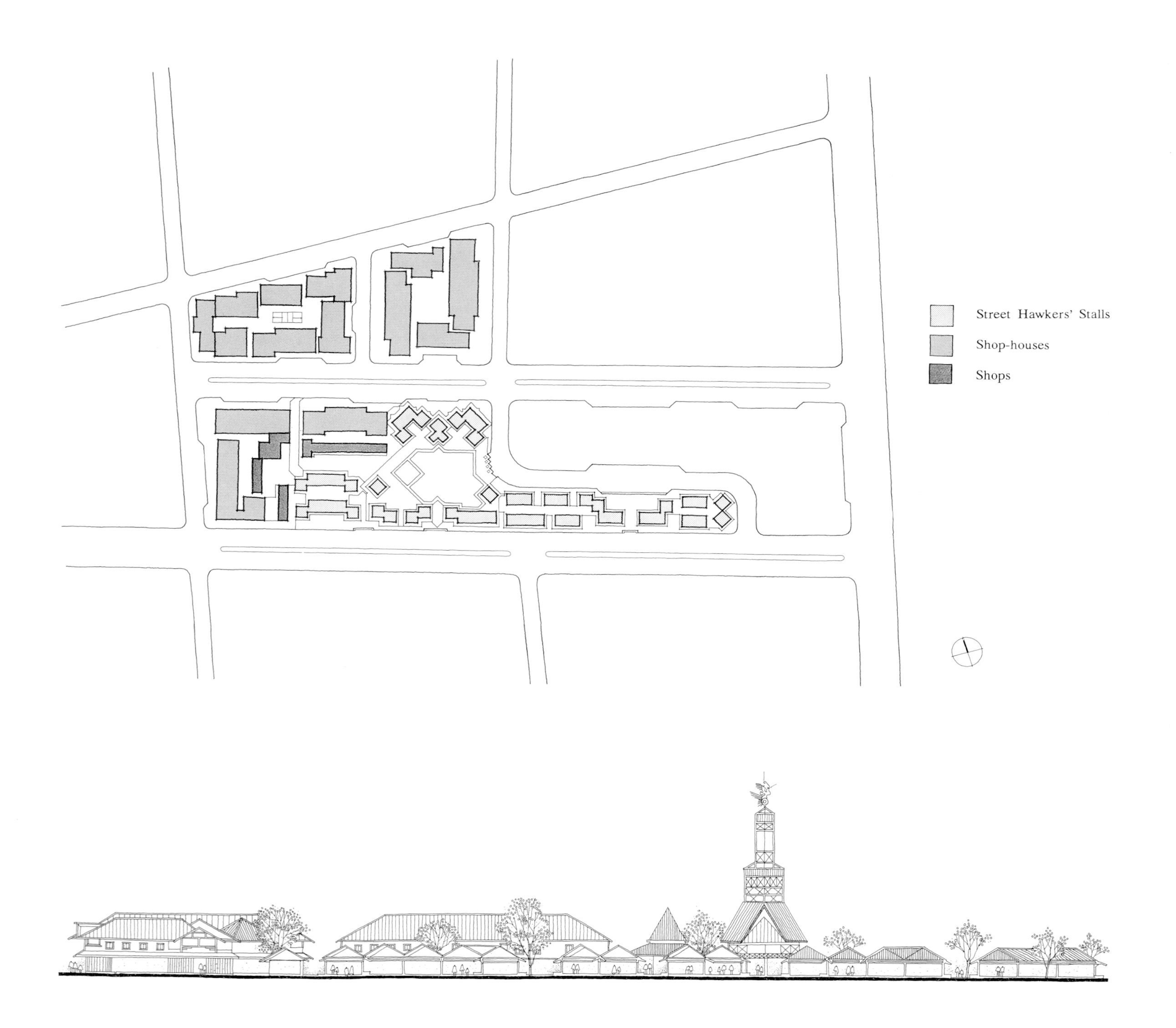
Street Hawkers' Stalls
Shop-houses
Shops

– the creation of innovate, complex financing schemes through a mixture of 'cross subsidy', 'self finance', self generating funds', 'resource financing', and basing them on a risk management basis;
– the creation of a profitable business which would include the social and ecological costs;
– the creation of a mixed use and integrated development scheme consisting of housing, commercial and recreational facilities;
– the division of the project into phases to make the financing viable.

The functional requirements of the brief, for both the designer and the developer, were clarified only after lengthy discussions that lasted for three years with the users and the Government. The principles that evolved were that all classes of users would have the same rights, land use must be mixed, and the design must reflect local style, and be physically attractive. Furthermore the layout between the buildings should be such that integration for all users will be easy, while rigidness of design should be avoided.

The developer defined the following types of users for marketing the complex: house-shop owners (high and middle income levels), kiosk-corner shop owners (low income level) and pavement trader-informal sector (lowest income level).

The programme was conceived in three phases with the first phase concentrating on a totally commercial development whose sale would finance the second phase, that relating to the informal sector. As the ratio of land use between the informal sector and others had already been specified by the Government, the developer had to work out the economics with great care. After all, thirty per cent of the built space in Phase I was going to users for free, while seventy per cent of the users had to purchase the properties and generate profit as the cross-subsidy. The building programme had to be computerised so that a sufficient cash flow and return was available.

The phasing of the number of retail outlets for the three types of users was planned as follows:

Phase	I	II	III	Total
House-shops	58	27	56	141
Kiosks	–	25	54	79
Pavement-trade shops	–	224	–	224

From the chart above it can be seen that the informal sector was given its facilities all in one go in Phase II, and that the developer was willing to wait until Phase III, when the commercial ratio is highest, before getting his final returns. It was a risk he was willing to take because he was sure that property values would rise after Phases I and II, and his rates would be much higher. It paid off handsomely. He was very particular about the kind of retail activity that should be allowed outlets, and only permitted six types of activities in the informal sector. Out of a total of two-hundred and twenty-four shops, 40.6 per cent were garment and sewing, nine per cent were in general merchandise, 17.4 per cent coffee and drinks shops, seventeen per cent food, six per cent shoes and leather work, three per cent medicine shops and seven per cent others.

Other facilities included in the design of the project were: a symbolic tower to act as a focal point for the site; public toilets; *bale bale*, or an open space for evening gatherings; a space frame, a covered space for performances; a car park; and a new traffic road, for construction between Phase II and III.

Meanwhile the designer, Antonio Ismael, was also working on a number of different fronts, integrating and coordinating the different aspects of the project design. From creating a festive atmosphere, and bazaar-like public squares, *alun alun* and *bale bale*, for the commercial and recreational benefit of the community, to a pedestrian design keeping vehicular traffic to the periphery. Cluster development for the commercial street hawkers and the shop-houses had to be designed to reflect the traditional *goteng royang*, or mutual aid lifestyle. Land sharing had to be worked out for playing spaces, garbage collection, fire safety as well as nursery facilities and planting. Pocket parking areas had to be distributed to avoid 'parking deserts'. Urban art had to be provided with a setting so that the ambience was civilised and cultured, and reflected the spirit of the society.

The project site area covers 2.7 hectares. The total built-up area of all three phases is 18,300 square metres (1.83 hectares) plus 1,800 in the informal sector. Open space and pedestrian ways take up 9,500 square metres, while roads take a mere 1,120 square metres. The break down of the built-up space is as follows: shop-house area covers 16,870 square metres, kiosks take up 1,443 square metres, and the informal sector occupies 1,800 square metres.

Therefore, in the final scheme, the informal sector gets 8.5 per cent of the total built-up area. The complex has double- and single-storeyed buildings. The former consists of a house above the shop and is sold as single units. Kiosks are single storeyed and have pyramidal roofs.

The building system uses wooden piles for the foundations. This is a common, local practice which is appropriate to the swampy soil conditions. Building superstructures are made of concrete columns and beams, while the kiosks are made of *ulin* wood. Most of the roofs are made of concrete tiles; only the street hawkers' stalls are covered with wooden shingles. Exterior wall infills are of fired bricks, while the interior of the residential spaces uses plywood partitions. Floors are made of both concrete and wood. The sanitary system uses double chamber septic tanks. Most of the open spaces, the plaza and the parking areas use concrete block pavers in which partial rain water can be returned to the soil via natural seepage. In fact, the entire building technology is local, as are the building materials.

The project was conceived in 1983. Two years later, in September 1985, the licence for building construction was granted, and by 1986 commercial spaces were already up for sale.

Total costs for the project are difficult to calculate but the basic costs are as follows:

TOILET

Phase I	Rp 1.1 billion	US $1,746,000
Phase II	Rp 1.3 billion	US $2,063,000
Phase III	Rp 1.5 billion	US $2,380,000
Total	Rp 3.9 billion	US $6,189,000

Other costs, such as resettling those who did not want to stay in the project came to Rp 0.4 billion or US $634,000. The interest costs were Rp 160 million or US $253,000. When one includes taxes, the total cost was probably around Rp 5.3 billion.

In Phase I the sale of the shops paid for thirty-eight per cent of the *kaki lima*, or the informal sector facilities. In Phase II the percentage came to eighteen per cent, while in Phase III the percentage rose to forty-four per cent. The total extent of cross subsidy was 13.2 per cent. It was found that labour costs came to approximately twenty per cent, with the material costs making up the remaining eighty per cent. Professional fees were 6.5 per cent, while project management fees came to 4.5 per cent respectively, of the project cost. The developer got a rate of return of twenty-seven per cent before tax which is high, despite the gross subsidies of Rp 700 million (US $1,111,000). He borrowed money from the State Bank which at one time exceeded forty per cent of the project cost, at a twenty-one per cent interest rate.

The cost per square metre of built-up area was Rp 289,000 or US $458. Two years later the cost per square metre for similar buildings rose to Rp 425,000 or US $674.

The maintenance for the project is carried out by a self-managed board with representatives from all the users. The service charges, parking fees and toilet fees generate an annual income of Rp 124.5 million (US $198,000), whereas the maintenance expenditure comes to Rp 114.5 million (US $181,000). The service charges for the *kaki lima* of the informal sector come to Rp 1,500 (US $2.5) per day. This, when broken down, works out as Rp 200 for the government, Rp 72 for rent, Rp 200 for electricity, Rp 200 for water and Rp 828 for the Management Board. This is very favourable to the *kaki lima*, who before the project, were paying Rp 2,000 a day in extortion fees, and another Rp 1,000 a day for water.

The Citra Niaga project is situated in the centre of Samarinda and it has become the focus and pride of the town. It is a well-conceived, well planned and aesthetically beautiful complex of buildings with a unique character and style. In terms of planning, it has succeeded in giving Samarinda a city centre. People gather here in the evenings, the young looking for entertainment, the street hawkers selling their wares, the shops, and the houses all generate activity that attracts and distracts.

The architectural achievement of the project is immediately visible to the visitor. What is not so obvious is the way the project galvanised the whole community into running the project successfully. It is not so easy in the developing world to obtain the cooperation of the different and disparate members of a community, and the fact that they did so is the most impressive achievement of the Citra Niaga project.

The commitment of the people who evolved this project is evident. The developer, Didik Soewandi who undertook the risk, and Antonio Ismael, the architect and catalyst, who visualised the whole development, need to be singled out for praise. The unusual system of using the commercial price of the big shops to subsidise the construction of the public areas and the pavement hawkers was so effectively worked out that all users profited from it. The achievement of a mix in retail outlets has given the project such an enormous dynamism that it becomes a complex market. A large choice is available for the visitors who can choose from expensive restaurants to fast food counters, and from boutiques to pavement clothes stalls.

This complex experience is traditionally and intrinsically a very Asian one, and should be encouraged. Too many new developments in Asia are looking towards the American model of a shopping mall whose orientation is merely profit. This exacerbates the already existing division between the rich and the poor, or the suburban wealthy from their own city's slum areas. In Citra Niaga, the developers have successfully managed to create an environment that reflects and encompasses the trades of all aspects and classes of a city, and in a profitable manner, which is obviously no mean feat.

An example of the colourful variety of shops included in the scheme; OPPOSITE: The use of tiled roofs on the interior of larger structures, while not functionally necessary, adds to their village-like quality

GÜREL SUMMER RESIDENCE

ÇANAKKALE, TURKEY

Client: Guzin Gürel, Istanbul. Architect: Sedat Gürel. Completed: July 1971

The summer residence of the Gürel family was built by the late Sedat Gürel for the enjoyment of his family and friends. The family normally resides in Istanbul but decided in 1968 that they would like a summer place in the Çanakkale region. They had spent many enjoyable holidays in that region and wanted a house of their own. The climate and setting suited them, and the wealth of historic and archaeological sites in the region was an added incentive for the family. Since friends and relatives frequently came to stay, the summer house had to accommodate numerous families and yet be able to provide privacy and solitude for individuals. Sedat Gürel acquainted himself with the ecology, climate and construction techniques of the local area, and conceived an architectural design consisting of several independent units.

The vernacular architecture of the Aegean and south-western coast of Turkey is conceptually Mediterranean. Whitewashed stone houses, cube-shaped, most often with a flat rather than a sloped roof, are the norm. Today most houses are constructed of brick, and have a wooden roof structure covered with tiles.

Turkish houses have a great deal of inbuilt elements in them. Rooms are provided with alcoves, cupboards, shelves, niches, latticed windows and sofas, all of which are built into the structure. The incorporation of these everyday utilities and objects into the vernacular architecture is a direct reflection of the aesthetic and functional convenience that is associated with Middle Eastern houses.

The objective of the Gürel residence was to accommodate the family and friends on a single site, on an area of about a thousand square metres, most of which slopes down to the beach. Seven sleeping and living units were designed, grouped around different courtyards, and resembling a small village. The first two units were for the immediate family of the architect; after his death they were occupied by his wife. Unit 1 consists of a sleeping area with its private bathroom and outdoor seating area, while unit 2 comprises the indoor sitting and dining rooms, kitchen, balcony and open courtyard. Unit 3 is equipped to house two guests, and has an attached bathroom. Unit 4 is much like the above, and was intended for the use of Sedat Gürel's parents. Since their death it has been used for guests. Units 5 and 6 were designed for Guzin Gürel's sister and family, and are similar to 1 and 2 except that they can sleep four people. The living unit (6) consists of

While unmistakably contemporary, the forms of the house echo those of local vernacular architecture; OPPOSITE: Built in benches, around a fireplace, contribute to the impression that the central court of the Gürel House is an outdoor room; OVERLEAF: Section; floor plan; a simple open trellis over one part of the court changes the character of this part of a relatively small space

0 1 2 3 4 5m
1
2
3
4
6
7
0 1 5m

a sitting and dining room plus kitchen, balcony and terrace making it a totally independent residence. Unit 7 houses the common services, garages and maintenance areas. Altogether, the total floor area of construction occupies 125.5 square metres.

Each of the units was designed and envisaged to be self-sufficient, and to be used independently. Privacy was ensured, but enough communal areas were incorporated into the overall plan so that it was still possible for the family to meet and gather together whenever they wanted to. Guests can feel free to come and go as they will, and to gather with their hosts in the many courtyards, or on the beach.

The open and rocky terrain around the units was left in its natural state. Dotting the landscape are numerous pine, olive and oak trees. Nature has been incorporated into the design process. The sea and sky, and the rocky landscape are integrated into the architectural format of the residence. There are numerous natural seating areas among the trees and rocks, and vistas of the sea and nature abound throughout the site. Nothing is intrusive. The individual balconies and courtyards offer the more controlled outdoors, but they too have been designed for a purpose, to funnel the sea breezes into the units. Footpaths and courtyards are paved with stones picked from the beach. Stone stairways, built into the rocks, lead from the units down to the beaches. A high wall, and a line of specially planted trees, help to insulate the residence from the traffic noises of the road situated along one side.

A simple traditional construction system using brick as the building material was utilised for the residence. Except for the woodwork, all major building parts were fabricated on the site. The technology was all local. Foundations were made of local stone, and the infill brick walls were constructed the local way. The roof was built on a wooden structure, and covered with terracotta tiles. Roughly applied whitewash was used to coat the exterior facades, and all the floors were tiled. Ceilings were made of timber, and wooden shutters were installed to protect the wooden windows.

The materials used in this house were of the simplest and cheapest variety, and available locally. The wooden furniture, doors, windows and shutters were made by a competent local carpenter, and display the simplest designs. Until 1971 there was no electricity in the residence. Lighting was provided by candles and kerosene lamps, water is from a well and there is no telephone. The Gürel family prefers and enjoys this natural life, and is not at all disturbed by the lack of modern facilities.

The architectural plan was completed in 1969, and construction began in September of that year. It was completed in July 1971, and the family moved in straight away.

The total cost of the residence came to TL 100,000, or US $700, the cost per square metre being TL 816, or US $57 (1971). All funds came from the Gürel family. The costs appear to have been below average for traditional contemporary constructions.

Maintenance costs are very low. The residence is only used during the summer; therefore, there are no heating costs. Fireplaces provide heat when and if it is necessary.
There is no cooling system, the wind from the sea being the most effective coolant. The units need to be whitewashed every two years, at a cost of some TL 100,000, or US $45 (1989), and the woodwork has to be painted and varnished every seven years. During the winter months the units are closed up but they can be opened, cleaned and ready for use in just a few hours.

All the members of the family and the guests who use the residence seem to be very satisfied with its performance. It provides them with a pleasant holiday setting which contrasts with their normally urban and busy life in the city. For a few weeks or months every year they are allowed the luxury of enjoying a beautiful haven in nature.

The Gürel summer complex, with its modest aspect, functions well. The height and size of the individual units, and their calculated and designed dispersal through the site, help to integrate them into the surrounding countryside. The separate units are insulated from each other, the wind blowing from the sea masking all other noises. The irregular disposition of the units offers a diversity of scenic views from many vantage points. The spatial unity of the whole complex is designed so that it seems to be in perfect harmony with nature around it.

OPPOSITE: In a grove of trees on the bluff above the Aegean, the various parts of the house give it a village-like aspect

HAYY ASSAFARAT LANDSCAPING

RIYADH, SAUDI ARABIA

Client: Riyadh Development Authority, Riyadh (Mohammed Al-Shaikh, President). Landscape Architects: Bödeker, Boyer, Wagenfeld & Partner, Düsseldorf, Germany (Richard Bödeker and Horst Wagenfeld, principals in charge). Completion Date: February 1986

In 1977 the Saudi Arabian Government decided to create a new diplomatic quarter for its new capital city in Riyadh. Its intention was to transfer all the diplomatic missions from Jeddah to Riyadh, once their new homes were completed.

The total area of the Hayy Assafarat (Diplomatic Quarter) comprises some five-hundred and eighty hectares of open desert land situated on the north-west outskirts of Riyadh, some eight kilometres from the town centre. The site stretches along the Daraiyah road over a length of three kilometres. It is bounded by Wadi Hanifah to the west. Topographically, the area can be characterised as a vast expanse of flat desert plateau with the precipitous escarpment, ravines, and the valley of Wadi Hanifah forming the only interesting physical features.

The climate of Riyadh is that of an arid desert zone with scanty rainfall, a high rate of evaporation, and summer temperatures that soar between forty to forty-six degrees centigrade, a characteristic of that type of environment. Vegetation is mainly scrub with tamarisks, acacias and palms being the only trees that grow naturally and with ease. All other cultivation and planting has to be carefully nurtured and sustained with irrigation.

The design for the Diplomatic Quarter was not only to include a residential area, offices and clubs, but also commercial, cultural and religious facilities for all the community. The landscaping of the whole area was judged to be of equal value and as significant as the architectural content and design. The architectural style of the central region of Saudi Arabia was taken as the reference for the study of the masterplan. Traditional patterns of Najdi architecture are evident in the urban design of the Quarter. There is easy accessibility between all parts with no great separation between the commercial, educational, public and religious facilities, they are all within walking distance of each other. Because of its novel approach the Diplomatic Quarter has become one of the most significant newly planned developments in the city, if not in the country.

Occupying a total of a hundred and fifty hectares, or about twenty-five per cent of the total developed area, the landscaping of the Diplomatic Quarter was arranged in two major categories, intensive and extensive landscaping. Both types of landscaping were conceived keeping the harsh desert climate

Map of the major roads in the Diplomatic Quarter, showing their relationship to the natural Wadi system nearby; OPPOSITE: Indigenous, low maintenance materials, used throughout the Diplomatic Quarter now provide a model for others to follow

well in mind, a hostile nature that had to be tamed and balanced, but not destroyed.

Intensive landscaping covers those areas that require irrigation (sprinkler or drip) and which form part of the design in both the private and public sections of the project. The area open to the public occupies sixty hectares of heavily planted and formally designed gardens, paths, walkways and playgrounds. There are altogether some seventeen public gardens varying in size from large neighbourhood gardens to tiny playgrounds. Extensive landscaping occupies ninety hectares of land mainly situated on the periphery of the built area, and which receives minimum water for irrigation. Earth berms and artificially created valleys or wadis and basins collect and channel surface water and run off from the roads into this arid zone. These extensive landscaped areas are linked to the rest of the open spaces by a network of green fingers and small gardens; they also act as transition zones between the planted and formal gardens and the naturally rugged landscape which surrounds the project.

The masterplan established the overall orientation for the landscaping, and concluded that the economising of water was to be the main environmental objective of the project. Any idea of a green and 'Westernised' garden with its lavish use of water was considered to be out of place. However, a 'green' environment, consisting of trees, fruits and other species, hardy shrubs, plants and flowers that would thrive in this arid climate, was thought to be essential for the overall image of the project. Street systems, roads and pedestrian networks were carefully designed to create a protected environment, shaded from noise, glare, dust and sand. Urban fringe areas were to be made to act as protective barriers against strong winds and sand storms.

All the landscaping designs were made to conform to the ecological and aesthetic requirements of the landscape. Microclimatic conditions were created by careful groupings of buildings and gardens. Trees were planted along all the streets, and pedestrians were provided with a network of walkways that would connect the different areas. Car traffic was to be strictly limited, and kept out of environmentally sensitive areas.

The basic concept of the masterplan was influenced by the lie of the land. The central spine which follows the contours of the land became the physical setting for the many embassies. The circulation routes and the major urban land uses were restricted to the flat terrain and surrounds of the allocated area. The escarpments and edges of the ravines and wadis, which provide such dramatic vistas of the surrounding countryside, were included in, and also helped to shape, the design of the layout.

Land that was unsuitable for urbanisation, land that was subject to erosion, poor slope and drainage, or bad soil conditions was set aside for extensive landscaping. Shortage of water resources was taken into consideration, and green spaces were clumped together for maximum versatility, maintenance and economic feasibility. Planted berms

A playful tent, with an artistic pattern revealed by sunlight in its interior, is a light-hearted gesture; OPPOSITE: A view of indigenous, low maintenance materials which are used throughout the Diplomatic Quarter; OVERLEAF: The blending of the natural and man-made elements indigenous to the region is characteristic of this design; a view from the rim of the escarpment at the western edge of the Quarter out to the Wadi Hanifah beyond; seating is incorporated into the natural stratification of rock ledges

alongside the roads and highways were the means envisioned to screen and protect urban areas from noise, air and dust pollution.

The date palm tree was taken as the main reference point for the Diplomatic Quarter as the ecological model symbolising all the attributes of the Najd. Even building heights were not to exceed the height of a palm tree. Nature and its ecological balance were to be kept intact by excluding animal grazing which had succeeded in destroying all living plants in an area of a hundred kilometres around Riyadh. State subsidies had allowed Bedouins to expand their herds and to indiscriminately dig wells and tanks; this short-sighted policy had effectively resulted in devastating the land.

Advised by the consultants, the client for this project agreed to use the project as a catalyst for restructuring the ecological balance of the area. Systematic seed collection of authentic plants from the deteriorated region was undertaken, and their replanting in the project nursery helped to recover more than three hundred and fifty species. Over two hundred and fifty animal and bird species were also saved and regenerated. The response from the people of Riyadh has been overwhelming. Thousands have actively become attached to the project, seeing it as a restoration of a code exemplifying their past way of life.

The formal aspects of the landscape designs, which included parallel lines of palm trees framing roads, well articulated earth berms, and rock formations that echoed and approximated the natural environment of the region also evoked an enthusiastic response from the users. Indeed both the local inhabitants and the transient foreigners of Riyadh use it with enjoyment. Other design features are also proving their success. Portals, seats, fountains, arcades and light fixtures were carefully thought out and made to specifically fit their location. The bench developed for the Quarter is now marketed world-wide as the 'Riyadh Bench'. Pavement patterns were designed around local themes and sensitively worked out.

Interestingly enough, the way that these gardens and parks are presently being used has provided a mirror image of the societies that make up Riyadh. Each nationality or group uses those parts of the parks or gardens that suit and reflect their way of life. Thus, the Egyptians, Syrians and Palestinians tend to congregate in Khozama Park, designed like an open oasis with generous lawns and terraces, and where their families can interact in a fairly unrestricted manner. However, the more traditional Saudi families go to Al Jajer Gardens where the ins and outs of the rocky limestone and desert-like configurations permit them to enjoy themselves, and still be able to guard the privacy of their tightly-knit families.

A rich variety of patterns and behaviours can be observed in these gardens, a variety that matches and reflects the diversity, the different social and cultural origins of the population of Riyadh. Family picnics, people jogging, bicycling and hiking can be seen alongside teams sports or contemplative people seeking seclusion and the view of the Wadi's edge. Mothers and their children use the playgrounds extensively. In fact, a remarkable encounter seems to be taking place between the people and the landscape of this new community.

In recovering hundreds of plants, animals and birds on the endangered species list, and allowing them to grow and have the freedom of this landscaped environment, the pioneering designers and consultants of this project have made a lasting and significant contribution to the stabilisation of the region's ecology. Not only have they reversed the process of desertification in that area of the Najd, but, even more importantly for the future, they have made a positive impact on, and shifted the awareness and consciousness of the urbanised population of Riyadh.

The earth berms and rocky landscaping give an ageless and lasting feeling to the parks, and as the vegetation continues to grow it will help stabilise and authenticate this natural look. Materials used for the pavements were all developed and made locally by growing local industries. The only intrusive new material used by the project designers is the metal tubing and mesh for the roofing of the arcades in the park.

Maintenance has to be continuous, and is particularly essential for the intensive landscaping areas. It appears to be under good control. Irrigation and drainage systems appear to be functioning well, and water wastage kept to a minimum. A micro-climatic condition has been successfully created.

The process and success of this project was due to the close working relationship of the client, the Riyadh Development Authority headed by Dr Mohammed Al-Shaikh, and the two principal landscape designers, Bödeker and Wagenfeld. The experience helped in building up the organisation of the Development Authority and in developing its capacity to deal with complex issues. In fact, the experience has allowed the client to develop an overall programme for national and regional parks, now in its early stage of implementation. Another and lasting symbol of this partnership was the creation, and the dissemination of knowledge for its maintenance, of a remarkable nursery, a repository for the local flora. Finally, the importance of educating the local people and the authorities, of opening their eyes to the fragility of their environment, cannot be understated. It will probably be the most important legacy of the Diplomatic Quarter.

OPPOSITE: The compatibility between new and existing land forms has helped to encourage use of outdoor areas; great care has been taken to make masonry features appear as natural as possible

AL-KINDI PLAZA

RIYADH, SAUDI ARABIA

Client: Riyadh Development Authority, Riyadh. Architect: Beeah Group Consultants, Riyadh (Ali Shuaibi and Abdul-Rahman Hussaini, Architects). Completion Date: November 1986

The Al-Kindi Plaza is located in the heart of the central area of the Hayy Assafarat. It comprises the basic cultural, religious, administrative and commercial facilities of the community. It also includes a Friday Mosque, a government service complex, a maidan or public square with shopping arcades around it, and a variety of gardens and restaurants. The total area of the site covers about twenty thousand square metres, while the total floor area is about fifty-four thousand square metres. The block, as a whole, is organised around the maidan, but each individual building is organised around a central courtyard. Two complex gateways link the block with the surrounding boulevards, filtering the traffic through the right channels – pedestrians through the ground floor while motor vehicles enter through the lower level where parking is available.

The urban architecture of the Najd was taken as the point of reference, and the Master Plan clearly shows that influence. Characteristic Najdi thick walls, small exterior openings, and the principles of seclusion and privacy are all evident in the design of the Al-Kindi Plaza. Response to climate and topography was also made to reflect the manner of local architecture. The sequences of the different spaces, souks, public squares and landscaped areas were juxtaposed in such a way as to create a semblance of older settlement patterns but without directly copying them. There is no doubt about the modern and urban design of the block.

The Friday Mosque, built according to a traditional Najdi design, dominates the maidan, forming one of its sides. Two tall minarets mark the gateways to the mosque. Shops, restaurants and other public facilities in arcaded buildings form one of the other sides of the maidan, while the government service complex completes the remaining defining edges. These offices are organised around carefully planted central atriums and a number of open courtyards. The atrium is used as a cooling space and also as an aide in communications between the different parts of the building, ensuring a rich and varied inner life behind the massive walls with their narrow openings.

The landscaping features of the Al-Kindi Plaza consist of shaded arcades, small fountains and other water elements, and planters. The maidan is paved with marble with a few plants placed along the sides. Absence of shade means that this public square is only used in the evenings. Traditionally,

The layout of the Diplomatic Quarter, organised into specific zones; OPPOSITE: In keeping with the traditional Najdi style, massive walls approximating the appearance of mud brick have few openings, as well as decorative triangular bands marking floor levels; OVERLEAF: This straightforward interpretation of Najdi architecture replicates the mud brick construction of the past in more durable, contemporary materials; two minarets identify the Friday Mosque, facing onto Al-Kindi Plaza

open spaces in hot, tropical climatic zones are only used after sunset, so even this design feature fits into the rhythm of the society. The Development Authority uses the office space available to it in an enlightened and responsive way. The general public has also been very receptive to this complex, and it is used intensively by people coming from Riyadh. They come to the maidan to pray in the mosque, to shop in the arcades, eat in the many restaurants or simply to cruise around. This is especially true on Fridays at prayer times, or in the evenings when open markets, souks and fairs draw huge crowds. The high quality of the design complex is not only romantic but also workable.

Most of the technology used for this project is a modern and imported one, a technology that is becoming increasingly more familiar in Saudi Arabia. Reinforced concrete was used in the framed system with hollow concrete blocks for the infill, the structure being of the monolithic slab and beam type. Some precast slabs were used in certain parts of the building. Insulated tiled roofs and suspended ceiling tiles complete the modern look. However, the external facades of the whole of the Al-Kindi Plaza were treated by spraying stucco on metal lath, creating a close proximation of the texture of the traditional mud plaster finish on adobe, formerly the most common building material used in the Najd. Imported marble tiles were used to floor the public spaces, and local cement was also used. Although all the interior enclosed spaces are air conditioned, many executives seem to prefer the natural and cool ventilation from the narrow openings on the outside wall.

An interesting concept for services and site utilities was provided through a central, linear tunnel which runs underneath the entire length of the site. It is accessible from the parking level and serves all the different elements of the centre. Independent entrances and exits were designed in a way so that they do not interfere with either the traffic or pedestrians. The contractors and the labour force used were mostly Korean in origin.

The total initial budget was SR 143.0 million and the total actual budget was SR 123.6 million, while the actual cost per square metre was SR 2,278. The architect claims that the cost per square metre was below that of the average building in Saudi Arabia; however, the land and infrastructure were provided by the Riyadh Development Authority. Construction began in April 1983 and was completed in November 1986.

The overall function of the Plaza seems to be very successful, and all the different parts work together harmoniously. Shopping arcades, the atrium and the controlled climates all seem to be functioning well. However, the most successful innovation in the use of materials is that of the sprayed stucco on the exterior facades. It creates a texture, shaded and unshaded, cutting out the glare and cooling the facades at the same time. No signs of ageing have manifested themselves yet; in any case the sophisticated and well disciplined maintenance techniques should be able to keep the buildings in good order.

FROM ABOVE: Arcades have various lintel heights to break the uniformity of column bays around the plaza; shaded, open arcades link all of the buildings in the complex; OPPOSITE: The Mosque, seen through the arcade surrounding the plaza; OVERLEAF: Planted gardens relieve the uniformity of sand coloured walls used throughout the complex; site plan; ground-floor plan; PAGE 102: Panels reminiscent of Kafess provide lacy shade along extended passageways; PAGE 103: The integration of landscape and architecture is a significant feature of this project

NO PARKING

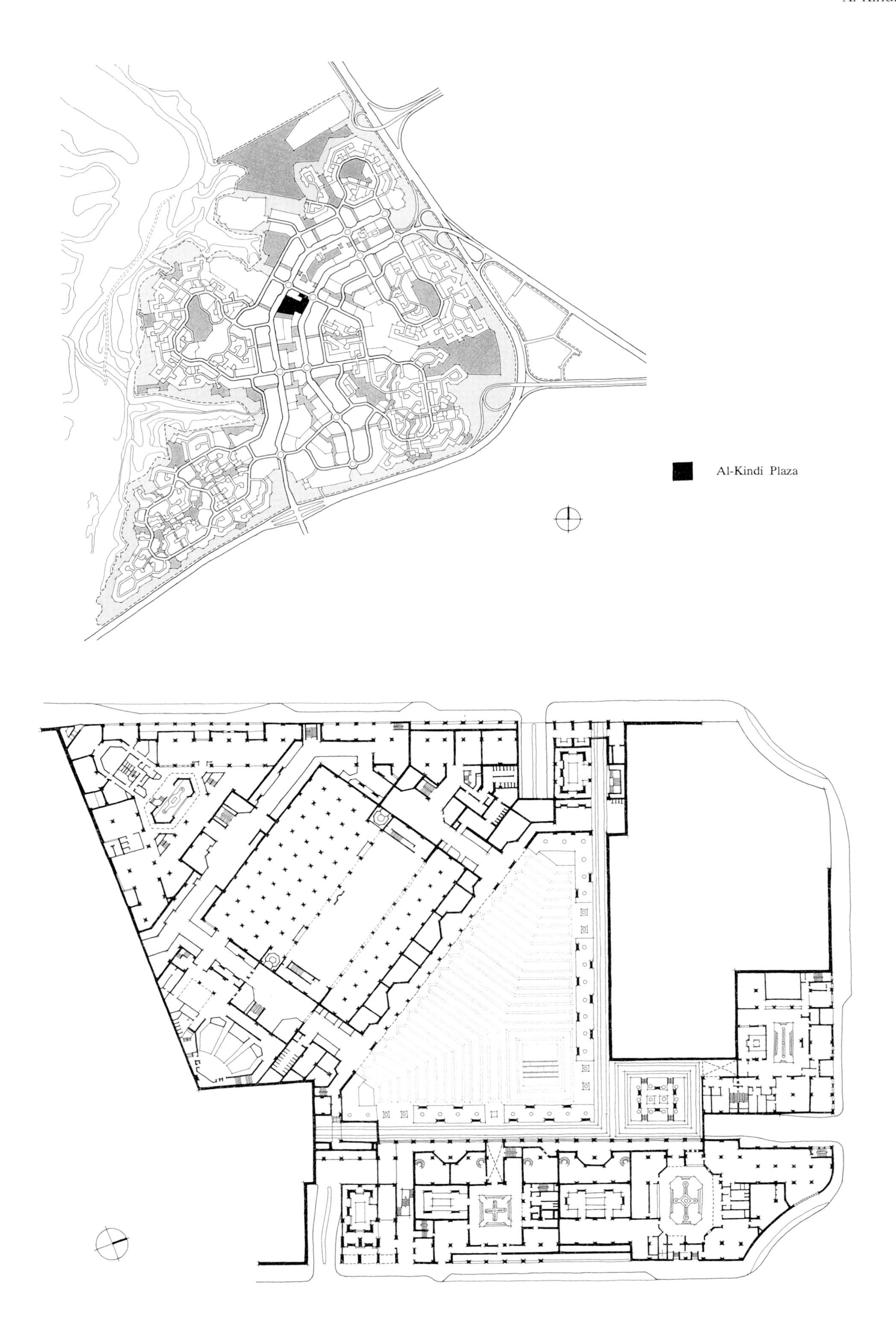
Al-Kindi Plaza

SIDI EL-ALOUI PRIMARY SCHOOL

TUNIS, TUNISIA

Clients: Ministère de l'Education Nationale, d'Enseignement Supérieur et de Recherche Scientifique and Ministère de l'Equipement et de l'Habitat (MEH), Tunis. Architect: Association de la Sauvegarde de la Médina (Samir Hamaici), Tunis. Completion Date: March 1986

Habib Bourguiba, the former President of Tunisia, used to work in an office located in the Bab Souika Halfaouine area. Many years after he became President he asked the Minister of Equipment and Housing to do something to improve that section of Tunis. The Minister was keen on the idea, especially since he wanted to help with rehabilitating and modernising the old medina.

Bab Souika dates to the eleventh century when commercial transactions with the nomads had increased to the extent that they overflowed through the walls of the old medina of Tunis. New areas were established in the open spaces outside the walls. By the thirteenth century two *ribats* had been formed, the northern one called Ribat Souk Souika and the southern one, Ribat Bab Djazira. These were complete communities with shops, work places and houses. The walls of these two *ribats* were linked in the sixteenth century to form the present day enclosure of the old medina of Tunis.

The Minister was enthusiastic about rehabilitating parts of the old medina by modernising them, and by setting up shopping malls, super markets and office buildings in them. The Association de la Sauvegarde de la Médina, established to protect and improve the old city, had different opinions about interventions that would change the values and the old fabric of the city. A compromise had to be found if the two parties were to be able to work harmoniously together to benefit the city.

The Minister appointed a Commission de Suivi which was to oversee the rehabilitation of the Bab Souika Halfaouine district. Over twenty projects were undertaken under the auspices of this Commission; Sidi el-Aloui was just one of them. The Commission designated the Association de la Sauvegarde de la Médina to design the school, providing that all decisions about the building, from the floor plans to the detailed specifications were first approved by the Commission. The architect chosen for the project, Samir Hamaici, was already employed by the Association. He faced difficulties not only with the Commission but also with the Société Nationale Immobilière de Tunisie (SNIT) which was the agency responsible for building all the schools in the country. SNIT followed a standard layout for all its schools, a linear building with a row of classrooms opening out on to a corridor. To convince SNIT and the Commission of the suitability of a new school design was an enormous challenge for the architect.

The vertical arched doorway, surmounted by a high window supported by brackets, has become the external sign for the school, as its main entry; OPPOSITE: While appearing quite restrained, the use of elements such as a mashrabiyya *over an arched main entrance, caused consternation among local building authorities, who initially tried to change them; OVERLEAF: The lean, open architecture of the interior is a dramatic contrast to the solidity of the outside*

The school is located in a dense urban area, close to the mosque of Saheb Ettabaa. It replaced an old school for the area which had been inadequately housed in the dilapidated Khaznadar Palace. The site is surrounded by low rise courtyard houses and narrow streets on three sides, and a park in front which abuts a main street, Rue Bab Bou. It is an elongated, flat plot of land left vacant after some residential buildings were pulled down to make room for a road that was to connect Bab Saadoun with Bab al Khadraa. Local objections saw to it that the road was never built. Instead, a third of the site was given to the (future) Sidi el-Aloui School, while the remaining two-thirds was landscaped, and turned into a public park known as Batha' Sidi el-Aloui.

The Ministry of Education, the members of the community, and the professionals represented in the Commission de Suivi had one main objective, and that was to build a school that could educate the maximum number of students. Quantity was given precedence over quality. The floor area for the school was so specifically given by the Commission that it curtailed the inclusion of many features considered (by Western standards) essential for a school. A library, gymnasium, diverse workshops, theatre and cafeteria are all missing from this school which has been designed solely for educational purposes and without any trimmings.

The architect, Samir Hamaici, who was born and raised in a traditional quarter of Tunis, is familiar with most details of traditional Tunisian architecture. As he was employed by the Association de la Sauvegarde de la Médina, which advocates the use of traditional forms, he proposed a courtyard building for the school. The design and drawings were completed in three months because the Commission wanted to complete the project quickly.

The design of the school respects the scale of the neighbouring houses. Even though it is more monumental it is not alien to its surrounds. In fact, the school's front facade resembles that of a house located opposite it. Hamaici also derived architectural details from the traditional environment of the area; the masses and height of the building, its courtyards, openings, decorations and colours, all reflect this assimilation. The architect has made the maximum use of the small site by building two rows of classrooms separated by a sizeable courtyard. The school contains sixteen classrooms, each 49.8 square metres (there are eight of them per floor), a large meeting room, 45.6 square metres, four offices each 4.2 x 4 metres in size, a small clinic, an art workshop for the pupils and a staff room. A three-bedroom flat, measuring a hundred and thirty square metres, and situated on the second floor is for the use of the headmaster and his family; this is a customary practice in all Tunisian schools.

From the outside the building appears as two masses separated by staircases, inside it appears as one courtyard divided by a bridge. Classrooms are distributed symmetrically around the paved courtyard. The school occupies the ground and first floors, the headmaster's flat taking up the second floor over the front gateway. Rectangular piers support the galleries that surround the courtyard. The main entrance is aligned with the principal axis of the public park, and is marked by a traditional *mashrabiyyah*, an ornate wooden window, above the door.

Landscaping is practically non-existent in the school. The courtyard is bare of trees, and only a few potted plants and flowers are distributed along the edges of the galleries. There are no benches, or sand pits for the children to play in. According to the Headmaster, the noise of playing in the courtyards would make it virtually impossible to teach in the classrooms. The bare surface of the courtyard apparently also helps to keep the school clean-looking. Apart from three paintings decorating the walls facing the courtyard there is no art, and no one is allowed to draw or place any objects in the galleries. The Headmaster keeps a tight control on the school; it is very organised and appears to be efficiently run.

The school serves the district of Halfaouine which has about ten thousand inhabitants. The official monthly income of a family averages between TD 70-120 (US $75-129). In actuality it is probably higher because there is usually more than one bread earner per family. Halfaouine is considered to be an upper low-income group. One thousand pupils use the school. They are divided into thirty-one classes, each class having between thirty-six to forty-two pupils. They range in age from six to twelve, and the ratio between boys and girls appears to be about even. There are two teaching shifts, so that the school is used from 7:30am to 5:30pm. The first group comes in from 7:30 to 10:00am, the second from 10:00 to 12:30pm; the first group returns from 12:30 to 3pm, and the second group comes in again from 3 to 5:30pm.

Given the financial restraints and the limited budget for this project, Hamaici managed to blend remarkably well the users' needs with the aesthetic qualities of the building. The architect, client and the community are all proud of the building.

A reinforced concrete frame structure with hollow tile flooring and hollow brick infill was used for the school. All the facades were rendered with cement; other surfaces were finished with cement plastering and then painted with white plastic paint. Doors, windows, and *mashrabiyyas* were made of wood by skilled local craftsmen. Window grilles for the ground floor, and the hand rails for the galleries were cast of wrought iron. Low priced red marble tiles were used on the edges of the galleries, and to mark out and define the courtyard.

All the materials were produced in Tunisia including the steel, electric wires, lamps and wash basins. Almost all the work force, skilled and unskilled, the consultants, and the contractors were Tunisians, the sole exception being a French architect who worked for the Association.

The climate of Tunis is of the Mediterranean type, hot and dry in the summer and rainy and cold in the winter. Average temperatures in January, the coldest month, are between six to eight degrees centigrade in winter, and thirty-one to forty degrees centigrade (when the southerly winds blow) in summer. It rarely snows. There are no heating or cooling

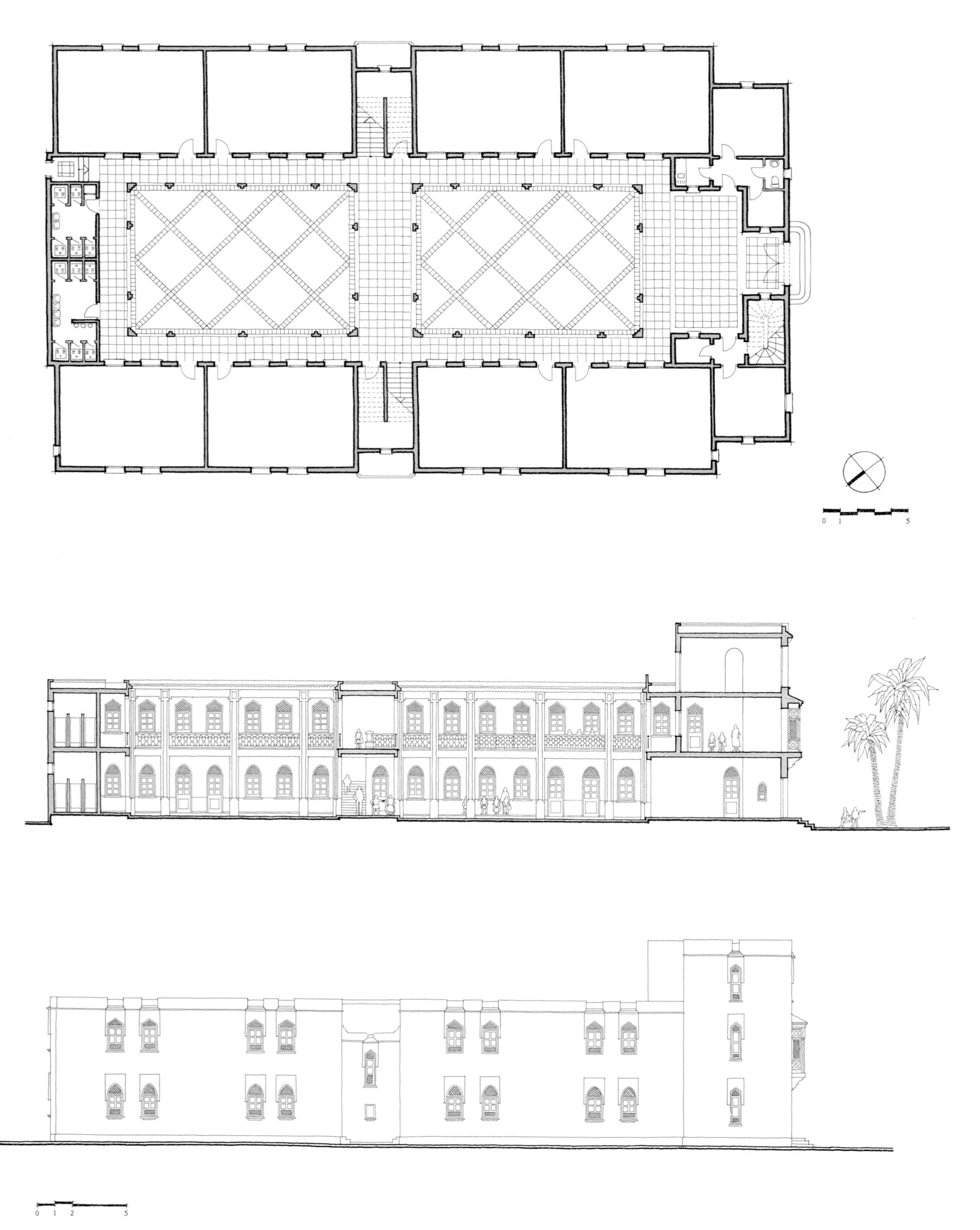
0 1 5
0 1 2 5

devices present in the building. However, the ceilings in the classrooms are high enough to create enough space for hot air to be ventilated through the upper part of the windows, which keeps the rooms cool enough. Presumably body heat suffices to keep the temperature at a comfortable level during the winter months. Each classroom has five windows, three onto the courtyard and two onto the street. Sixteen fluorescent lamps in the classrooms help to improve the light for the students in the afternoons or during dark and wintery days.

The cost of a typical school built by the Ministry of Education is TD 220-230 (US $237-248) per square metre, whereas the cost of constructing an average quality housing unit is TD 350 (US $377). The cost of the Sidi el-Aloui School came out to be TD 241 (US $260) per square metre. The total cost of the school was TD 465,000 (US $501,078), with most of the funds coming from the Ministère de l'Equipement et de l'Habitat.

Although it cost more than the average Tunisian school, the quality of the workmanship involved is much higher. In fact the architect himself supervised the construction work, making sure that all his details and designs were executed properly.

The design for the project was started in March 1985 and ended in May 1985. Construction began immediately under the direction of the Ban Ayad and Jebali Construction Company. Once the foundation stone was laid in March 1985, the school building took one year to complete. It was inaugurated with a ceremony in October of that same year.

The building integrates well with its surroundings, and it has not yet shown any signs of ageing. The spaces are well articulated, and the circulation patterns are simple and effective. The courtyard idea is pleasant to look at, and the columns add an elegant air to that space. The sole problem with the building seems to be its acoustics. The classrooms, situated opposite each other across the courtyards, generate a lot of noise. This is augmented by the noise of the street outside. Closing the windows in the classrooms is one solution, but this cannot be done in summer. If it is, cross ventilation will be blocked and temperatures will soar inside. Acoustic tiles, carpets or at least curtains may help to reduce the noise level.

The innovation of this school building is that it is the first to be built using an original design. It does not follow the normal plan of schools in Tunisia. In respecting the constraints and limitations of the site and the budget, the architect took enough of a challenge upon himself. Add to that the preservation of the architectural integrity of that area of the old medina, and the challenge increases for the architect. Yet Hamaici managed to produce a landmark building that is traditional and modern at the same time, thus refuting the argument forwarded by those who are against using the past as a reference because it stands against progress. He has created a modern school that fulfils all the requirements of an educational establishment yet, at the same time, reflects the aesthetics of the architectural heritage of the old city of Tunis.

Colour, where used, is muted and subtle; OPPOSITE, FROM ABOVE: Ground-floor plan; longitudinal section; northwest elevation

CORNICHE MOSQUE

JEDDAH, SAUDI ARABIA

Clients: Municipality of Jeddah (Mohammed Saïd Farsi, former Mayor) and Ministry of Pilgrimage and Endowments, Jeddah. Architect: Abdel Wahed El-Wakil, London. Completion Date: 1986-88

During the last ten years, the Egyptian architect Abdel Wahed El-Wakil has designed more than a dozen mosques in Saudi Arabia. The first of these mosques, the Sulayman Mosque, completed in 1980, caught the eye of Mohammed Saïd Farsi, the Mayor of Jeddah, who then commissioned him to design a mosque along the corniche of his city. The Ministry of Pilgrimage and Endowments followed suit, and commissioned another one along that same corniche. A series of mosques were commissioned by these, and other, sponsors from the private sector.

The mosques differ widely in size, composition, and budgets but they have a number of characteristics in common. They are all revivalist in style, their architecture deriving from a blend of Islamic vocabularies but relying most heavily on those of the Mamluks of Egypt, and of the neighbouring Rasulid Dynasty in Yemen. They were all designed within the short span of six years, and belong to one period – art historically speaking. All are located in two cities, five in Jeddah and two in Medina. Both cities are situated in western Saudi Arabia, in the province of Hijaz.

Jeddah's topography is flat, its climate coastal and tropical. High levels of humidity, and even higher temperatures make it an uncomfortable city to live in. Rainfall is minimal, and the soil is unsuitable for agriculture. Landscaping the urban fabric and turning the desert into gardens has only been possible through the importation of soil, and by desalinating sea water from the Red Sea. Historically, the city's importance was established by the Caliph Othman who chose it as the port for Makkah in AD646. It evolved into a cosmopolitan commercial centre, catering to goods and pilgrims from all over the world. Its traditional architecture reflects the style of the Red Sea, with some overlying Egyptian and Ottoman influence. Intense building activity since the 1960s has destroyed most of Jeddah's old city centre.

Medina is a very important city for Islam, for it was here that the prophet Mohammed established the first Islamic state. His house, mosque and tomb are located in this city. It lost political significance after the Caliph Ali moved the capital to Kufa in Iraq in AD656, but remained a major religious centre. During the yearly pilgrimage, or Hajj, it is visited by an estimated two million Muslims from all over the world. Most of the old city has been destroyed by expansive rebuildings, while its old mosques have been enlarged

FROM ABOVE: Elevation; at the seminar held following the Award Ceremony in Cairo, the architect compared the Corniche Mosque to a Mamluk predecessor, which was its model. Such historical prototypes consistently make up a valuable design resource in El-Wakil's work; OPPOSITE: Architect El-Wakil utilises delightful surprises, such as this view of a minaret, seen through a gap between a seafront arcade and the main prayer space to punctuate procession

beyond recognition. Medina is located in an oasis, it has fertile soil, and it is famous for the fruits of its orchards. Its topography is fairly flat but there are hills in the vicinity. It is cool in winter, and hot in summer. Rainfall is slight, and limited to the winter months.

The Saudi mosques of El-Wakil can be grouped according to their size into three types. The small mosques include the Island, Corniche and Binladen mosques in Jeddah. They are small mosques which do not exceed four hundred square metres in area. They were conceived as sculptural statements to decorate Jeddah's landscape, and were placed in areas where there had been no previous mosques, providing the many visitors and picnickers to the popular Corniche Beach with a place for their prayers.

The Corniche Mosque is like a pavilion open to the natural elements. Its striking views of the sea, and its openness to the sea breezes, made it such a popular place with picnickers during week-days and holidays that the site was overwhelmed. The Ministry felt forced to seal it off with a steel fence for its protection. It is now only open at prayer times, being most used during Friday's prayers. Functionally, the mosque works well, but its open design has rendered it susceptible to the harsh weather of Jeddah – the humidity, the sea, salt and wind have taken their toll on the building. The mosque receives little care, the plaster needs repainting, the wooden rails and doors suffer from chipping, and the chain of the chandelier was rusting so badly that it was removed by the Ministry and replaced by neon track lights. In spite of constant sweeping the floors are always covered with sand. Later additions such as the steel gate, a concrete annex for the keeper, public toilets, and a water tank have not helped its general appearance. In spite of these maintenance problems the natural setting of the mosque, with its simple and crisp forms set against the striking backdrop of the Red Sea, makes it a powerful image in a city of concrete high rises.

The Corniche Mosque, derives its name from its situation along the corniche of the Red Sea. It is built on land reclaimed from the sea. The site measures some twelve hundred square metres, and the mosque covers a hundred and ninety-five square metres of that area. It was commissioned by the Municipality of Jeddah. Although small in size, this mosque has a complex and formal arrangement. It is entered from the *qibla* side through a large and vaulted chamber. A change of direction allows entry into the building proper – through an open narthex which separates the prayer chamber from a two-bayed portico overlooking the sea. An external stairway on the southern side leads up to a minaret with squat proportions and a tall square base which supports a short octagonal shaft. Care has also been taken with the design for the keeper's lodge and the water tank and toilets.

The total cost of the Corniche Mosque came to SR 1,500,000 or 7,690 per square metre (US $2,000 per square metre). Although it was commissioned by the Municipality of Jeddah it was paid for with funds from private contributors. Begun in 1983 it was completed by 1986.

FROM ABOVE: Counterpoint, of vertical against horizontal, and rectangle against circle, is an intentional design principle which has been consistently used throughout the series; the arcade of the Corniche Mosque, which provides framed views of the Red Sea; OPPOSITE: The majority of the mosques in this series are built in clay brick, covered with plaster, which makes them glisten in the bright sunlight near the Red Sea; OVERLEAF: A slice of sky seen through an opening between arcade and prayer hall in the Corniche Mosque; PAGE 115 LEFT, FROM ABOVE: Section; floor plan; RIGHT FROM ABOVE: View toward the mihrab in the Corniche Mosque, showing the massiveness of the walls, which helps keep the interior cool; one step signals the change from the profane to the sacred

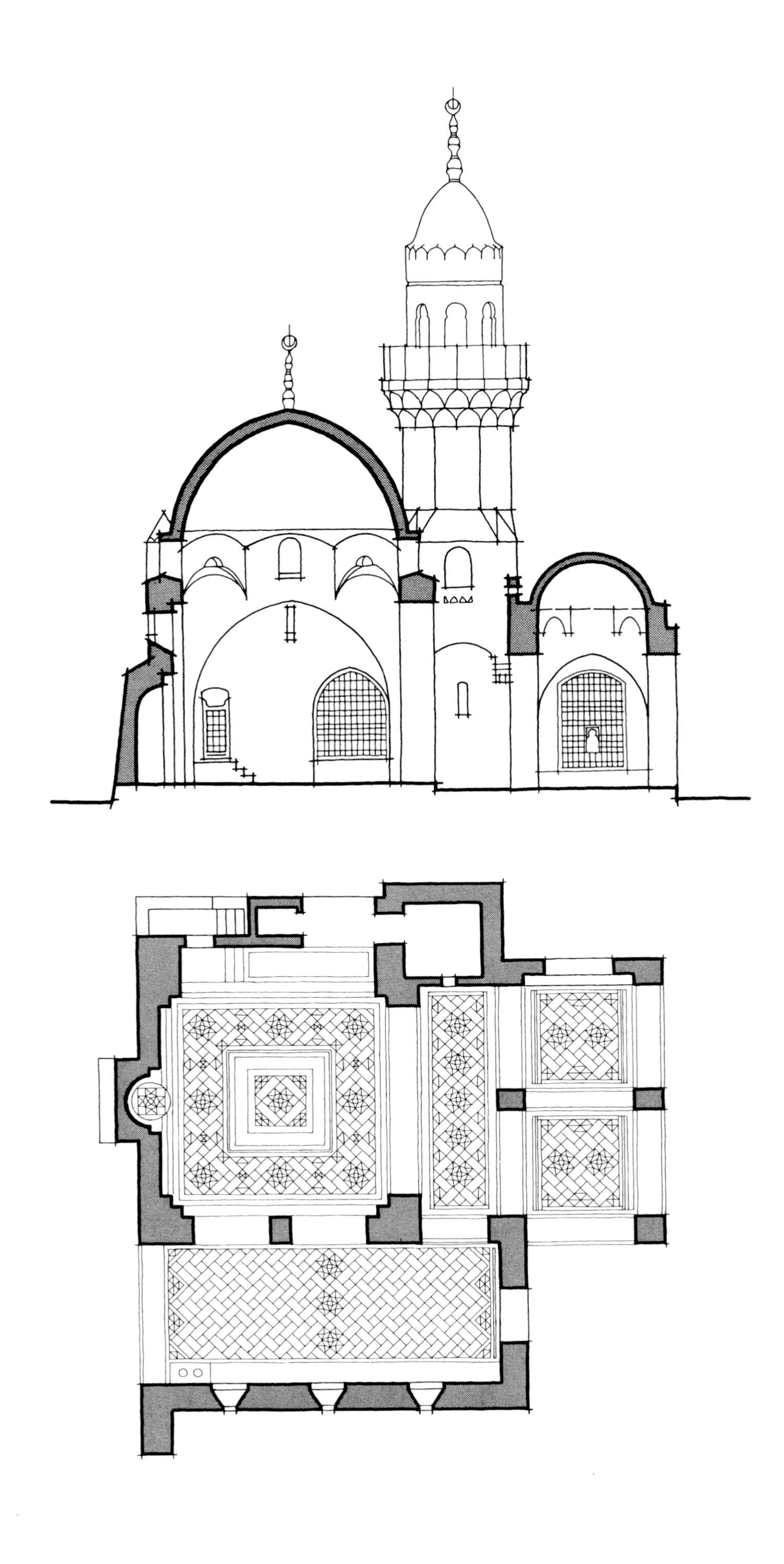

MINISTRY OF FOREIGN AFFAIRS

RIYADH, SAUDI ARABIA

Client: Ministry of Foreign Affairs, Riyadh. Architect: Henning Larsen, Copenhagen, Denmark. Completion Date: August 1984

During the last two decades the Saudi Arabian Government has slowly been shifting its seat of government from Jeddah to Riyadh. All the ministries and foreign embassies were moved, the Ministry of Foreign Affairs included.

The tender/programme for the design of this Ministry was formulated on the basis of a publication entitled *The Ministry of Foreign Affairs: the Organisation Development Plan* which was approved by the Cabinet in 1977. An architectural competition was organised in June 1979 with the help of the Union Internationale des Architectes. The Master Jury included Hassan Fathy as well as the Minister and his deputy. Eleven designers were invited to participate and present their designs. They were: Piano and Rice (Italy); V Dalokay (Turkey); T Dannat and Partners (UK); P El Khoury (Lebanon); R Fairburn (USA); F Otto (Germany); A Isozaki (Japan); R Taillibert (France); Taller de Arqitectura Bofill (Spain); Suter and Suter (Switzerland) and H Larsen (Denmark). The building was to include the following:

- 85,000 square metres of office and circulation space to be divided into three sections: political, cultural and administrative affairs;
- main offices for the Minister and his deputy;
- a banquet hall, mosque, library, conference centre, exhibition space and training facilities for the diplomatic corps and a consular section;
- extensive parking spaces sufficient for eleven hundred employees and many visitors.

The competition went through two phases, and four candidates were short listed. Henning Larsen's winning project used the historical and architectural context, continuing with past traditions, but he placed the building firmly in an international and modern idiom.

Riyadh is situated in the eastern desert zone of Saudi Arabia, and is the traditional centre of Saudi dynastic power. It was a small town before the oil boom with two-storeyed mud buildings, structured around central courtyards, the adobe walls giving the city its distinctive ochre colour. The street facades were windowless and rarely decorated.

The climate is hot and dry. Temperatures may reach forty-seven degrees centigrade in summer, and rarely fall below twenty degrees centigrade in winter, although occasionally they go as low as zero. Rainfall varies but the annual rate averages about 11.5 centimetres. It is usually dry and humidity

FROM ABOVE: Semicircular forms, flanking the main entry, contain the library and a diplomatic school; a sloped ramp-stair assists pedestrian entrance into the Ministry, and blends in well with the solid exterior; OPPOSITE: Octagonal light-wells punctuate the processional sequence into the secluded central court at the heart of the building; OVERLEAF: Sharp shadows reinforced the crisp lines and plain surfaces of the building's exterior; PAGE 120: A long, low profile was intentionally chosen by the architect, because of reduced heat gain

rarely reaches fifty per cent. Prevailing winds in winter are from the south, while in summer they are from the north. Sand and dust storms are a major problem in the city.

The site occupies a whole block in the al-Namodhajiyah quarter. Once considered the outskirts of the southern part of the city, it lies eight kilometres from the Diplomatic Quarter, and two kilometres from old Riyadh. Riyadh is one of the fastest growing cities in the Middle East. It is modelled on the pattern of a low density American city with cars as the prevalent form of travel. It therefore has a modern and dense network of roads.

Henning Larsen wanted to incorporate the basic principles of Islamic traditional design with contemporary architectural language. He especially wanted to use the idea of a courtyard, considering it an indispensable element of Islamic building design. Anonymous and blank facades, as well as a clear hierarchy between the private and public spaces were also considered to be of prime importance. The whole physical mass of the building's structure had, of course, to appear to be homogeneous.

The interior of the building is organised into three spatial areas: the entrance/lobby sequence, the square/street sequence and the courtyard/offices sequence. The building has a low and compact shape, rising by three to four storeys. Its square plan is missing one corner which is meant to symbolise the embassies abroad. The building is constructed on a raised platform, somewhat after the style of Indian Muslim Architecture. This houses the garage. Its massive aspect and blank facades reflect the traditional aspects of old Riyadh houses. Its sober exterior offers a sharp contrast to the richly decorated interiors of the courtyards and inner streets which emulate the intricacies of an Arab house.

The main entrance is monumental, and is located along the diagonal axis of the square. It is flanked by two massive cylindrical towers which house the banquet hall and the library, both of which are easily accessible to the public. The central access is pedestrian. Entry is affected through a large and vaulted gallery which leads directly into the main lobby. There is no doubt about the majestic character of this space which rises impressively through four storeys. The whole sequence is solemn, formal and official. The lobby is lit by strips along the edges, and by hanging bulbs which give the illusion of traditional mosque lamps.

This central lobby is surrounded by a triangular street which is covered by three-storeyed barrel vaults, the idea inspired by traditional covered souks. At each corner of the triangle are octagonally shaped domed areas, the so-called 'squares'. These streets and squares provide access to the reception rooms, offices, stairways and other services. The streets are paved with attractive green and white marble tiles laid in a chequered pattern. Small openings in the vaults provide the light for these streets which are cooled by fountains and water canals.

Three octagonally shaped squares form the centres of the individual block units, each block being structured around three courtyards; these provide the flexible office space. Offices for the Minister and his deputies are located on the top floor of the main facade. Each block houses one of the three main departments. The courtyards are square in shape and divide into three types: the cross garden, the fountain garden and the water basin garden. Each type is in a different colour, and each has distinctive patterns of tile pavings that help accentuate its identity.

There are three main gates from the front road. The gate on the main axis is used for state occasions, and two gates about sixty metres equidistant from the axis are for daily use. A gate on the north side acts as service entrance for trucks and other deliveries, while one on the east side is used for consular services.

The Ministry has a double external wall with a small air cavity between. The exterior brownstone veneer is Crema Mora from Italy while the interior wall is made from concrete slabs. The construction stands on reinforced pad and strip foundations. Columns and beams are of prefabricated steel, while the floors are made of a composite steel decking and a 8.5 centimetre layer of concrete. The construction grid is 7.2 x 4.8 metres. The roof is insulated with marble/concrete tiles, and the interior walls are covered with gypsum board and painted white. Off-white acoustic plaster covers the interior street ceilings. The floors of the public spaces are paved with green and white marble tiles, while the offices are covered with neutral coloured carpeting. Patio walls are painted in sophisticated blues, mauves and ochres.

Mechanical systems are very sophisticated. Security and fire monitors are controlled by a central computer and can isolate areas of the building. Air conditioning works on an 'algorithm' system whereby a computer regulates the humidity and the temperatures by constantly checking and anticipating exterior changes. To handle the dryness and the exceptional temperatures that last late into the night, a long cooling tank with a capacity of two thousand tons was installed. Small apertures, *mashrabiyyas*, baffled light slots, thick walls and high quality insulation all help to keep the building cool.

Nearly all the technology, labour, and materials comes from outside Saudi Arabia. The steel comes from Japan, and the mechanical systems are of mixed European origin (English, German, Swiss, etc). Electric lights are from Denmark, as is the white nautical paint. The spherical lights were hand-blown in Germany, and the crystal chandeliers are from Austria. The architect was, of course, from Denmark, as was the engineer, and most of the white-collar workers. Contractors worked with Saudi partners. The manual labour was mostly Korean, and ninety per cent of it was unskilled. Work on site continued on a twenty-four hour basis, with eight hour shifts. Approximately two thousand workers were employed on the site.

The programme was formulated in 1977-79 and Larsen was selected in the spring of 1980. Construction commenced in 1982, and was completed by September 1984, with a delay of only three months.

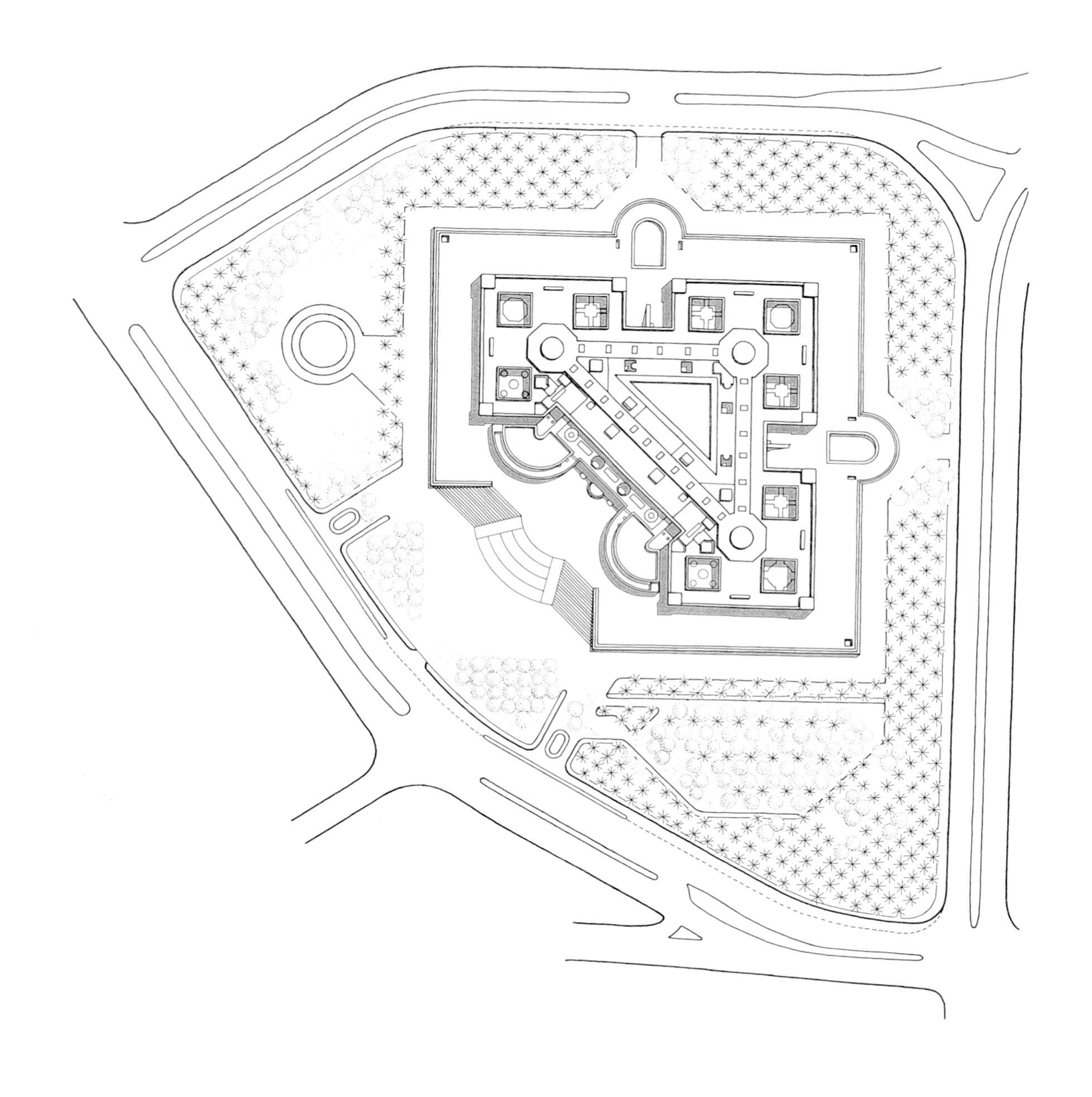

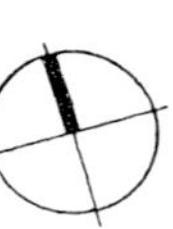

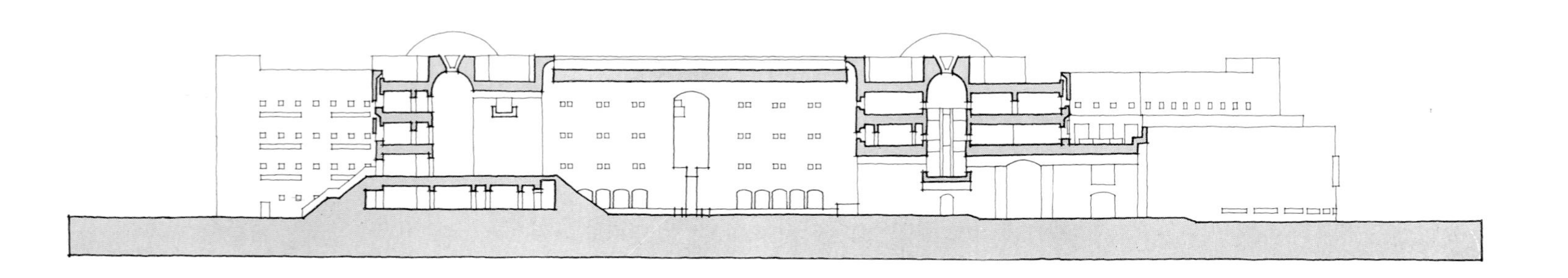

The total cost of the project, including the main contract, telecommunications, art works and furniture came to SR 615 million, or about US $150 million. Including the car park, this amounts to about SR 6,530 per square metre or US $1,600 per square metre. Other state commissions of the same period in Riyadh range from 1.5 to two times this amount per square metre. Funds came from the Saudi Government. Maintenance costs are a state secret.

The building appears to work well. The public spaces, monumental and lofty, evoke a delicate balance of dignity and ease. Circulation is clear and well marked, the streets and square are well lit, cool and quiet. Fountains and canals refresh the atmosphere. The offices are comfortable and of good dimension, and they afford a certain amount of privacy to their owners. A small area in the lower part of the building has been designed and set aside for the use of women.

The insulation seems to work very well, and the lighting is handled superbly throughout. The external materials appear to have withstood so far the harsh climate of Riyadh, and to have weathered the sand, wind and dust. The interiors are frequently repainted to maintain their pristine quality. There have been small leaks during strong downpours, and the patio walls do not have sufficient mouldings to handle exposure to water. Dust, however, is the main problem in Riyadh, and it remains to be seen how the gardens and fountains will be affected by it.

Not part of the completed design, some ornaments and panels, commissioned by the client and produced by Moroccan craftsmen, have been introduced into the building against the wishes of the architect. They contrast sharply with the pure and abstract conception of the building and its furnishings.

The Ministry of Foreign Affairs building reflects Islamic principles of geometry and composition. It is one of those rare buildings that has managed to successfully marry a traditional style of architecture with a modern vocabulary. It has taken the mud-mass of the Riyadh fort and turned it into a modern building of note. If nothing else, its soaring lobby with its vaulted streets and chequerboard floors remains imprinted as a magic space in the mind's eye.

FROM ABOVE: The quiet recesses of library carrels, used to read the rare manuscripts in the Ministry's collection; Henning Larsen was given the opportunity to visit many of the most important historical landmarks, throughout the Islamic world, and has incorporated many of the concepts he has seen in this project; OPPOSITE, FROM ABOVE: Site plan; section; OVERLEAF: Private courtyards, which are colour-coded to relate to their specific sector, to provide a place to talk privately outside the office; latticework pergolas are used to accommodate private seating areas in open courtyards

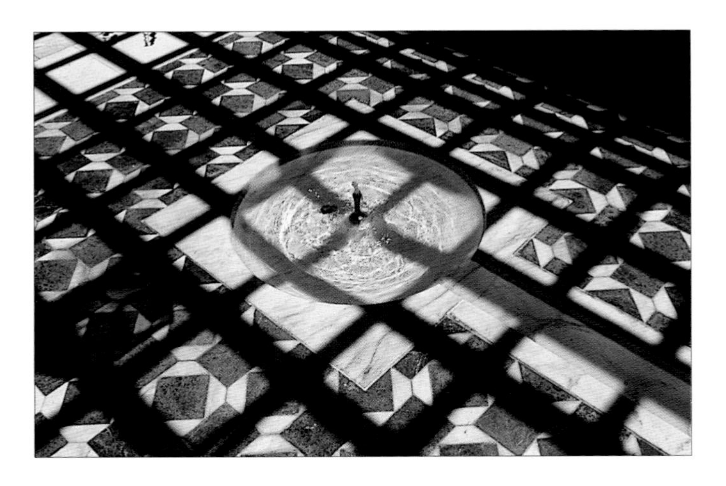

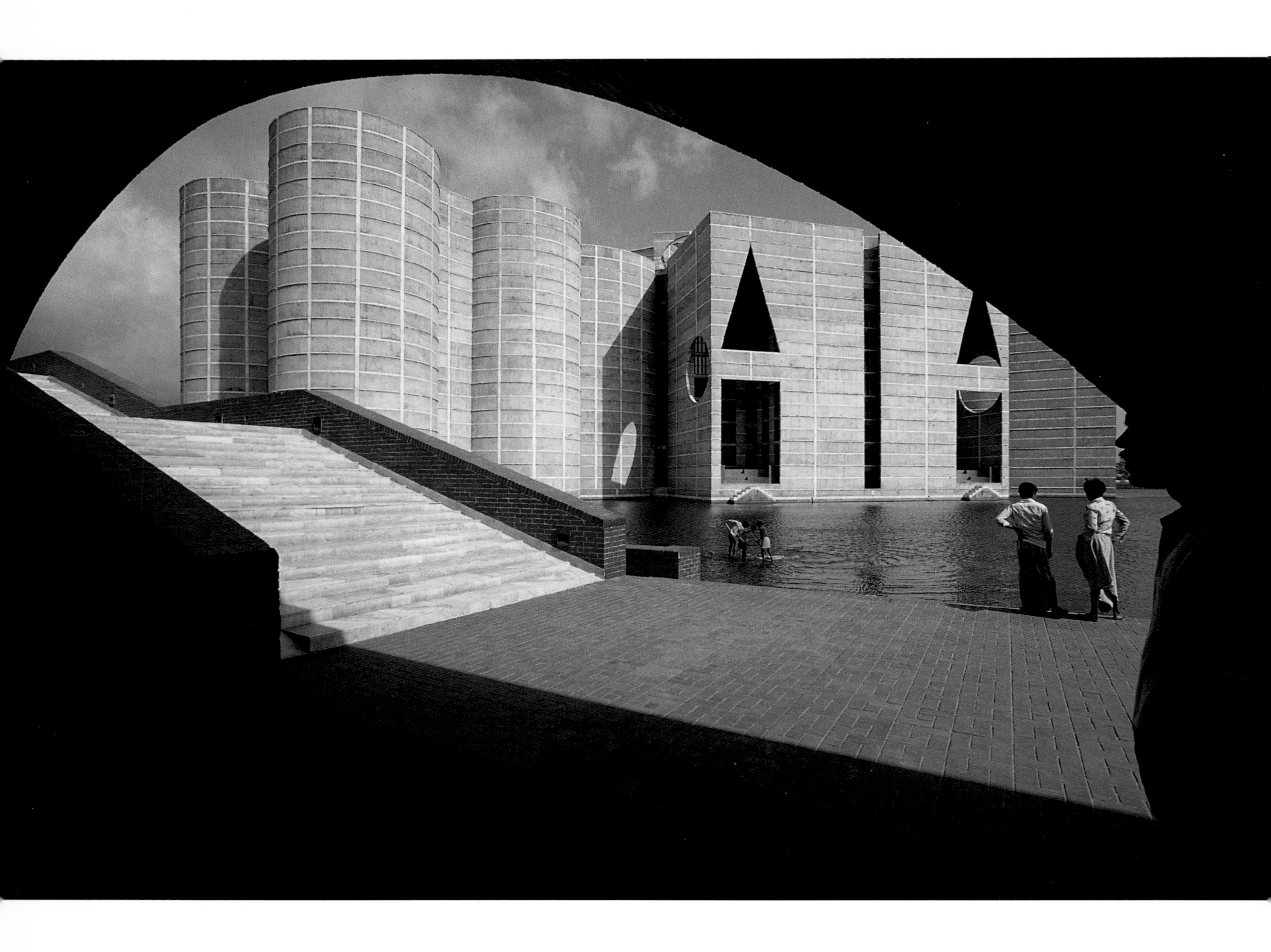

NATIONAL ASSEMBLY BUILDING

DHAKA, BANGLADESH

Client: Public Works Department, Dhaka. Architects: Louis I Kahn, David Wisdom & Associates (after 1979), Philadelphia, USA. Completion Date: July 1983

In the turmoil following the departure of the British the Indian subcontinent was divided into two separate states, India and Pakistan, the latter into two entities, namely East and West Pakistan. East Pakistan, dominated by its western partner, soon became a hotbed for the autonomy movement. In 1959 the government decided to establish a second capital at Dhaka in East Pakistan, an attempt at bridging the gap between the two. Each capital was invested with responsibilities which were supposed to be interrelated. The secretariat was set up in Islamabad while the general assembly was designated to be in Dhaka. However, the movements seeking independence continued to gain ground, and the ensuing repression from Islamabad sparked off the civil war in 1971. With Indian support East Pakistan achieved independence, adopted the name of Bangladesh, and made Dhaka its capital.

In 1962 Louis Kahn was asked to make studies and plans for a National Assembly which was to be sited in the 'second capital', Dhaka. It was to be a symbol of the democratic power and modernity of the state. Begun in 1966, the construction work was interrupted by the civil war in 1971 when only three quarters of the building was completed. Work resumed and by 1983, twenty years after it was first begun, the complex was completed.

Bangladesh is a vast plain in the delta of the Ganges and the Brahmaputra Rivers. Its huge population depends on the rivers, the monsoons, and the level of the waters for its livelihood. Its capital, the city of Dhaka, is located on the river Buriganga. It is an old trading town that came into prominence during the Mughal Period, when it became the seat of government for the province of Bengal. Dhaka rapidly developed into one of the great emporiums of South-East Asia. The construction of the railway in the 1880s turned Dhaka's business priorities inwards towards the hinterland of India, and changed its character forever. River traffic began to lose its importance and the river banks their prestigious position. Dhaka's expansion began to spread north of the railway line rather than along the river. The old town remained Indian while the new town became British, the towns separated by the railway tracks which acted as the demarcation line between the two. The new section of town, called Ramna, continued to grow with the Raj and after independence. At present Dhaka has as area of 324 square kilometres, and a population of four and a half million. When

The vertical scale of the exterior walls is modulated by thin strips intended to reduce the cost of cladding the entire surface in marble, and yet convey a sense of richness, as well as marking the lines where scaffolding would be set; OPPOSITE: Louis I Kahn saw this Assembly Building as his most significant project, intended to marry modernist principles with his regional sensibilities; OVERLEAF: Kahn was fond of castles, which are recalled here in the round towers at the entrance, and the moat around the entire building; the ways in which light is modulated in the corridor surrounding the main hall is characteristic of Kahn's concern about the necessity of having it pervade interior space

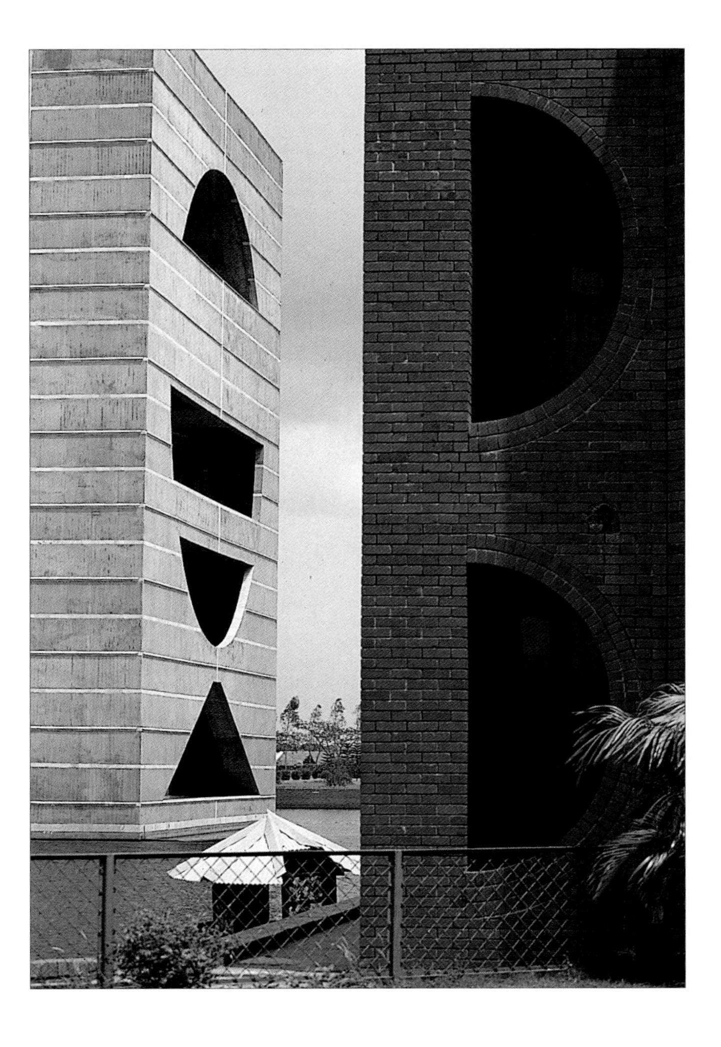

the Pakistani Government decided to establish a second capital and assembly at Dhaka they wanted a site distant from Ramna. The site allocated for the Assembly Building was seven miles north of Dhaka city centre, in a low-lying, flat plain. It covers an area of eight hundred and forty acres, and is oblong in shape. Louis Kahn had indicated that a thousand acres was the minimum amount of land required to meet the needs of such a monumental project. Of the eight hundred and forty acres that were allotted for the complex, six hundred belonged to the Government and two hundred and forty were privately owned.

The original brief called for a National Assembly building, as well as three hostels to house the ministers, delegates and other officials coming from West Pakistan. Other buildings and residences were also included in the programme. When the Republic of Bangladesh was formed in 1971, the new Government modified the plans, even though construction had been going on since 1964. The Assembly was expanded to seat two hundred and fifty to three hundred members, galleries had to accommodate five hundred visitors, plus another hundred for the press corps; a prayer hall, post office, commercial bank, library, restaurant, lounge facilities, a reception hall and offices for the President, ministers and other personnel were also added to the complex.

Kahn planned the design in five major components which were to be placed in a 'necklace formation'. These comprise the National Assembly block, the centre-piece of the entire project and containing nine blocks, the south block or main plaza, the Presidential Square, the east hostels, and the west residential block. The layout of the complex is based on a main north-south axis, with the Assembly Chamber acting as the focal point of interest and attention. This was achieved by designing a monumental building for the Assembly itself, and by placing the smaller buildings on diagonals to the east and west of it. A man-made lake, which they face, separates them from the secretariat.

The Assembly is in the form of a cylinder, in effect, a hollow concrete column with perforated walls. The 'column' is octagonal in shape, and there are eight sectors on the eight sides of the octagon. Against the eight sectors there are eight outer blocks. The nine blocks (including the central assembly block) interconnect only at levels one and three. The outer blocks are interconnected at even levels while the central block is connected with the central and eastern blocks at odd levels. The plaza entrance south block is not connected to the outer blocks at levels four and six. The 'column' is also used as a light regulating structure throughout the complex. Deep openings were cut out of the wall facades to protect the windows and to provide shelter from the wind and rain.

To the south, the prayer hall forms the entrance to the Assembly buildings. This linking resulted from the realisation that the meaning of assembly attains a spiritual dimension when applied to community participation, which is what any Islamic community does when it goes to the mosque. From the north, the complex is approached through the park and

The 'moat' accentuates the verticality of the Hall, which is reflected in it; OPPOSITE: The powerful forms of the Assembly Hall rise up from the flat plain surrounding it; OVERLEAF, FROM ABOVE: The geometric openings in the exterior wall have caused some controversy in the past, but are consistent with what Kenneth Frampton has identified as Kahn's rationalistic leanings; the offices on the perimeter of the building are private, with a view over the water

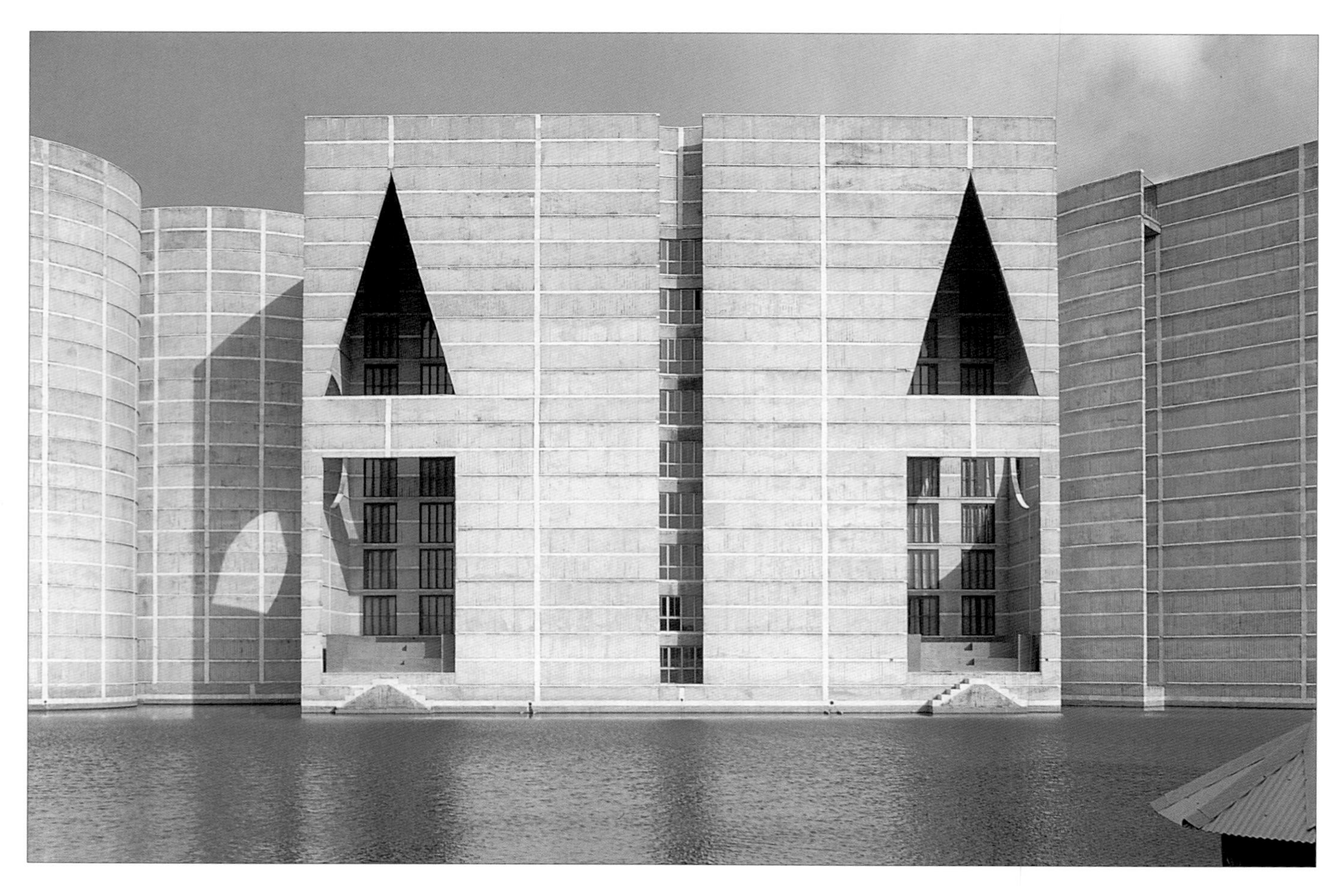

Presidential Square. Facing the Assembly to the north is the Secretariat, with offices, halls and National Library. The hostels and dining halls are sited along the edge of the triangular lake looking towards the Assembly. Housing for the civil servants is to the west of the hostels. Covered walkways connect all the hostels to the Assembly. The hospital occupies the north-west sector of the complex. Vehicular traffic access is from the south.

Kahn successfully used water in his landscaping design for the Assembly grounds. In a country that sees too much of water in the form of floods and rains, he managed to overcome the prejudice felt by many, and demonstrated that the control of water is what is important. His walled lakes are interconnected with drains and canals in a system that collects and channels the rainwater away from the site, and into the river.

The design process was influenced by local architectural styles, and especially by Islamic pre-Mughal and Mughal architecture, especially the Mausoleum of Humayun in Delhi, the Red Fort at Agra and the Lal-Bagh Fort at Baharpur. Roman baths and pantheons were also studied, and the effects of the beaux-arts are also represented in the complex. In all, the design embodies a synthesis and interpretation of many cultures, endeavouring to be a symbol of universalism.

Before the complex was started, before even the design process began, Louis Kahn established an office in Dhaka. He initiated a research programme to better understand local architectural styles and the traditions of building, and to evaluate the climatic factors that influence the city. He experimented with numerous techniques which later helped him to establish the methodology for the construction of his complex.

Kahn wanted to use modern man-made materials that were imperfect, and to hide those imperfections with a perfect material, marble. His research team worked out the best type of forms for pouring concrete, how they were to be built, held in place, and be stripped without the necessity of rubbing or patching. It was determined that the tallest practical dimension for one day's work would be five feet, and this became the standard vertical unit of dimension of the whole building. Kahn accepted and liked the irregularities of vertical wood forms, but he did not like the cold joints left by placing one day's concrete directly on top of the previous day's work. So he devised a recessed joint, six inches high. These joints, placed at five foot intervals, created a design out of a necessity. Their recesses gave him a precisely formed horizontal edge both on the inside and on the outside. The cold joints and tie holes were covered by marble inserts which were set in place later. The marble inserts on the exterior are alternately shaped with a projecting drip moulding and a plain face. On the inside, the marble insert became a base at the floor line, and a band course halfway to the next floor. The floors are finished with terrazzo tiles with marble dividers, borders and bases.

The Assembly building is constructed in rough-shuttered, fair-faced concrete inlaid with bands of white marble, the latter mask construction joints and incorporate drip mouldings. Piling is Franki piles. Reinforced by bearing walls with masonry arches and reinforced concrete ties were used for the hotels and hostels. The reinforced plain, ribbed or coffered slabs were left exposed. This was the first major building complex in Bangladesh to use concrete as a building material.

All the hostel buildings, the houses, and the outpatient departments are made of reinforced brick masonry-bearing wall construction. Since Bangladesh has abundant supplies of silt-rich clay, brick has long been a traditional and popular building material. It is both durable and inexpensive. In the recent past it has been supplanted by cement or concrete blocks which are faced with a stucco plaster. For the last century, stucco has been the most common facing material in Dhaka, but it peels and goes black with the monsoon and requires frequent whitewashing. Exposed brickwork, however, requires a minimum amount of maintenance. Kahn wanted the exposed brick work to be the only form of decoration, and so he meticulously designed sample walls, joints, arches, and stairs which were to act as the models for complex. They all had to meet his high standards. He even built a sample building in Dhaka which still stands.

Lighting in the Assembly Chamber was designed to be effected by a combination of diffused natural and artificial light.

Maintaining a consistent illumination level, a balance between the natural and the artificial, has proven to be a problematic issue in the building. There are similar problems with the lighting in the prayer hall. Acoustics have also proven to be deficient, and there have been many complaints about echoes and reverberations, especially in the Assembly Chamber. Many of the areas that were intended to be naturally ventilated had to eventually be air conditioned, including both the mosque and the Assembly Chamber. This has added to the cost of the upkeep and maintenance of the buildings, and it is an extra load on the electricity system of the city.

Some of the design features have also been a problem. The first and foremost being the complexity of the design which, especially for people unaccustomed to the layout of the buildings, causes disorientation. The intricate circulation patterns, as well as the complex vertical and horizontal orientation of the buildings adds to the confusion. Employees suffer because they feel that they have been cut off from the outside world by the massive concrete skin that envelops them. It is a building that is inward by nature. Its enclosed spaces are foreign to the local population which is used to open, low buildings with deep verandas, high ceilings and large windows.

Architecture in humid zones is designed to admit breeze, and keep out the sun and the monsoon rains. Louis Kahn's building is only partly effective in responding to the local climate. The climate of Dhaka caused many problems for the complex as a whole, but especially for the four office wings with their deep window openings. The wind driven rain was

so frequently of such a destructive force that the windows had to be covered. This was done with pre-cast concrete and panels of glass tiles; a violation of Kahn's rules. The original timber windows did not weather well and warped. They had to be replaced by aluminium frame windows. The heavy rainfall in Bangladesh was not correctly anticipated by Kahn, and rain has penetrated parts of the brickwork. The large openings while good for ventilation are bad for windswept rain.

Its overall unfinished form of construction, the concrete facade, does not show any major signs of ageing.

Some of the facilities attached to the complex are not being used for the purpose for which they were designed. The hostels, built to house members of the National Assembly, are now occupied by the staff and families of the military administration. What was to be a hostel for government officials functioned briefly as family residential quarters during the military rule of General Zia. It has now been divided into three civilian areas of accommodation: firstly, for non-residential MPs, from rural areas, who come to stay for the session; secondly, permanent accommodation for residents of the Dhaka constituency; and thirdly for civil servants.

It is difficult to evaluate the total cost of this complex since its construction spanned a period of more than twenty years. In 1962, Louis I Kahn was selected to be the architect for the masterplan of this project. In 1964 an agreement was signed, and construction work began. By 1970 the work had already begun to slow down because of lack of funds. In 1971 civil war broke out, and East and West Pakistan became separated. Work on the complex was suspended. On December 16th 1971, Bangladesh received its independence, and the concept of the Capitol Complex changed to that of a National Assembly. Work on the building recommenced. In 1974 Louis Kahn died, and the Government engaged the firm of David Wisdom & Associates to secure the continuity of the design principles. Work progressed, and by 1982 an assembly session was held in the building. The completion of the project took another year.

The Public Works Department is unable to give exact figures for the total cost of the complex, but the sum of TK 1,332,38 million, or US $53 million has been quoted (in 1983). Today, an average building in Bangladesh would cost about US $260 per square metre. The building of the Assembly cost US $650 per square metres in its day. Whatever its true cost, the budget for the National Assembly complex is largely surplus to that of any other construction undertaken in Bangladesh. The entire project was paid for with government funds.

The annual maintenance and operation costs of the building was estimated by the Public Works Department to be TK 52.43 million, or about US $2 million in 1983. This includes the cost of the electricity, water, sewerage, landscaping, and the salaries of the maintenance staff. This is an enormous annual cost for a country to support, especially one that has other urgent social and economic priorities.

The same language of openings, used on the building exterior, is carried over into the corridor walls; OPPOSITE: The corridor in the Assembly Building was seen as more than a functional circulation space, and recognised, in scale and profile, as the place where political decisions are actually influenced; OVERLEAF: The semi-circular form of the Assembly Hall stems from the architect's belief in the concept of gathering, as an elemental human institution; ground-floor plan; site plan

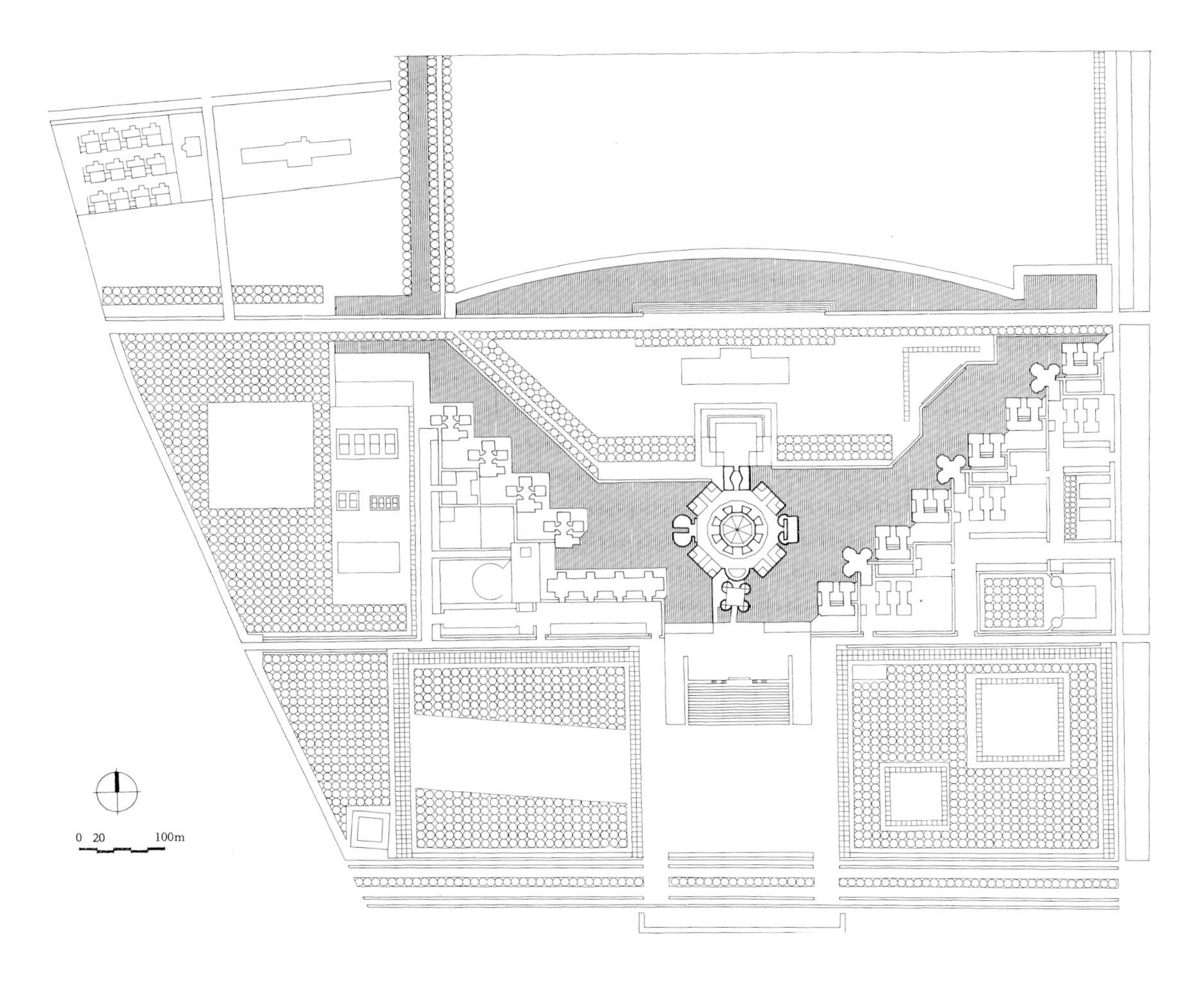
0 20 100m

Louis Kahn's grand and powerful concept for a National Assembly in Dhaka dominates its setting like a fortified citadel. Its symbolic and aesthetic impact on the landscape is undeniable. In spite of the upheavals that the country suffered through the twenty years that this monumental complex took to be built, it did build it.

It required an enormous local effort to keep up with the design and the high quality of the construction techniques required for the project. The fact that it was finally completed is a testimony to the commitment and the enthusiasm of the Bangladesh Government, the Public Works Department, and the construction workers. They justifiably express and manifest enormous pride in their ability to have undertaken and completed such a monumental enterprise. It has become a model for the pursuit of excellence in the architectural community, and a symbol of the country's desire for social and technological progress.

The National Assembly has had a direct hand in helping the formation of the country's first school of architecture, inaugurated in the 1960s, and that of the Institute of Architects of Bangladesh, created in 1972. It encouraged the renaissance of architecture as a profession, and that in a country where most of the building work is carried out by untrained individuals or construction engineers. It influenced students, and directly helped to produce talented architects. It also gave a big boost to and encouraged the building trade.

The two basic materials, concrete and brick, that were used in the construction of the Assembly were shown at their best. Although concrete is too expensive a material for the majority, the use of bricks flourished. In Dhaka alone eight or nine new brickworks have been built, and this has opened up a new job market. The building of the National Assembly also benefited the workers and local craftsmen. The skills and experience gained by them on the construction site has equipped them for many other projects in the region or the Middle East.

The National Assembly is considered unanimously by the inhabitants of Dhaka to be an important complex, a landmark in modern architecture. They are proud that it is in their city. They look upon it as a unique building endowed with national and international significance, and making a positive contribution to the culture and the environment of Bangladesh. Even the political opposition is in favour of this complex; its high cost is justified as a symbol for the betterment of the future.

Throughout the political, social and economic turmoil of the past decades, the people of Bangladesh have been able to sanely and wisely differentiate between the human and social concept of what this complex represents. For individuals aspiring to justice and democracy the Sher-e-Bangla Nagar complex stood as the symbol of an attainable and tangible ideal.

By its virtue as great quality architecture the National Assembly created an overall awareness of innovation, composition, and design in the country. Its original synthesis of traditional culture and heritage with a totally modern spirit and design has created a new and contemporary identity in Bangladesh. The genius of Kahn, his geometric order and the complex mathematical values of his design, like those of a many-faceted precious stone, permeates the building.

It has attracted international attention, and an Aga Khan Award. In spite of the huge costs, the people of Bangladesh are justifiably proud of their National Assembly, and consider it an investment in their future.

FROM ABOVE: Kahn's enlightened rationalism is most evident in the Pythagorean logic of his forms; by recreating in concrete the ubiquitous parasol, used by Bangladeshis to protect themselves from the sun, Kahn has not only demonstrated his virtuosity in this material, but also his keen sense of observation and belief in metaphor; OPPOSITE: Looking towards the rostrum in the Assembly Hall

INSTITUT DU MONDE ARABE

PARIS, FRANCE

Client: Institut du Monde Arabe, Paris, France. Architects: Jean Nouvel, Pierre Soria and Gilbert Lezénés with the Architecture Studio, Paris. Architectural Consultant: Ziyad Ahmed Zaidan, Jeddah. Completion Date: November 1987

The Institut du Monde Arabe, or IMA, is one of the large scale projects to have been built in Paris during the last decade, a new architectural landmark, heralding Paris of the year 2000. Situated in the centre of the city, the building provides a meeting place for the two cultures that produced it, France and twenty Arab countries. Its aim was to change and correct the poor image of Arab culture in France, and to reinforce France's understanding of that part of the world.

Officially the idea for the IMA goes back to 1980 when the twenty founder states signed the foundation charter of the Institut. These states included Algeria, the UAE, France, Iraq, Jordan, Kuwait, Lebanon, Mauritania, Morocco, Oman, Qatar, Somalia, Sudan, Syria, Tunisia and Yemen (both North and South); Libya did not join until 1984, and Egypt also joined later in 1989. It was established as a French foundation of public utility, and subject to French law. According to the agreement, the land was to be donated by France but the building costs were to be financed by the Arab countries. The responsibility for the administration and financing of the IMA was given to an Executive Committee of twelve members, six French and six Arab. A High Council with thirty-six members was also established.

The first site allocated for the IMA was in the fifteenth arrondissement. It was turned down by the residents of that neighbourhood. In 1981, the Minister of Culture, Jack Lang, selected the new site, in the historic fifth arrondissement. This site was culturally and historically more prestigious; its location in the oldest section of Paris and facing Notre Dame conferred upon it a special significance.

Seven young architects were asked to submit proposals for the competition. They included Roland Castro, Henri Ciriani, Edith Girard, Yves Lyon, Jean Nouvel, Gilles Perraudin and Christian Portzamparc. They were given three weeks to present their architectural plans for the site. Jean Nouvel's novel and hi-tech solution won the day.

The site for the IMA is an impressive one. It is bounded by the urban fabric of the nineteenth century Boulevard St Germain to the west, and the more modern Jussieu University buildings to the south. But it is the north front that demands true attention, and makes the site a privileged and exceptional one. Here, facing the River Seine, and with the profile of Notre Dame in the distance, was the challenge of a lifetime for any modern architect.

FROM ABOVE: Steel and glass prevail on the majority of the Institut's exterior walls; translucent alabaster panels elegantly diffuse natural light; OPPOSITE: Steel stairs reinforce the hi-tech image that pervades the Institut; OVERLEAF: The Institut has taken its place alongside many prestigious neighbours on this segment of the left bank

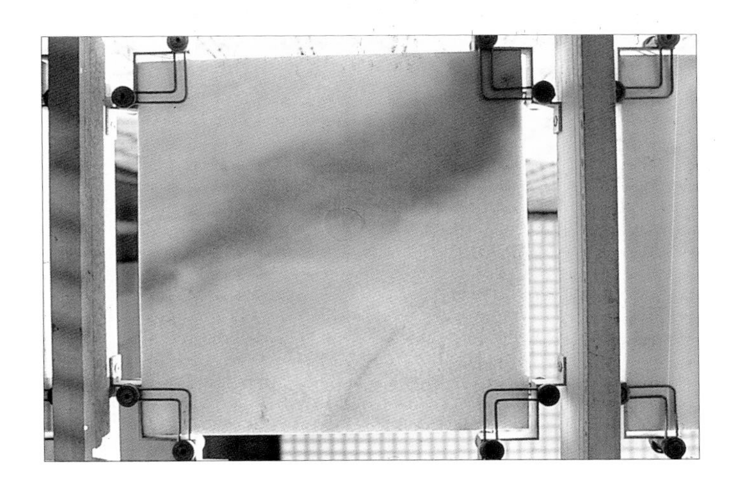

Jean Nouvel tackled the project by presenting a neutral face masked by curtain walls. The mass of the IMA is divided into two wings with a cut between them created by a narrow east-west slit ending in an interior court. The building measures seventy-seven metres in length, thirty-five metres in width and is thirty-two metres high. It is nine storeys high, and contains museum and exhibition halls, a library and documentation centre, an auditorium, a High Council Hall, offices, a restaurant and cafeteria, a roof terrace and a car parking garage. It has a large open square, a *saha*, to the south, in which the already existing trees formed the only landscaping.

There are two entrances into the complex, one from the river bank in the north, and the second from the square in the south. The lower floor houses the exhibition, plenary, and Hypostyle halls as well as the auditorium. The car park is built under this floor. Two vertical elements, the elevators and staircase in the south wing and the service and sanitary units in the eastern section of the building, rise through the upper floors. The library which is located in the south-western part, goes from the first to the sixth floor. Its spiral staircase, resembling a minaret, can be seen from the outside through the buildings's transparent skin.

The Museum has been so arranged as to occupy levels going from the first to the seventh floors. The different ceiling heights and diversified levels add to the visual effects of the exhibition space. Administration and office spaces are also on various levels, on the first, fifth, sixth and upper floors. The director's office and the High Council Hall are on the ninth floor. A cafeteria in the north wing of the roof terrace offers spectacular views of the Right Bank and the islands in the Seine. The interior spaces of the IMA are juxtaposed at all levels. Most of the spatial and functional units are interconnected with each other, the glass and metal see-through effect visually uniting the interior spaces.

From the outside the building is a study in comparisons. The pointed end of the north wing contrasts sharply against the tall and narrow rectangular front of the southern section, the two divided by a thin slit, a metaphoric cul-de-sac. The contrast continues in the appearance of these two facades, both curtain walls but treated in very different ways.

The north facade, facing the Seine, is bow-shaped and has a polished look, better to reflect the architectural skyline of the river embankment opposite. Continuous aluminium frames horizontally divide its polished facade, and act as a curtain wall hiding and negating the interior divisions of the building.

The flat southern facade is made up of two hundred and forty square grids. They function like diaphragms on a camera shutter, metallic irises which filter the sunlight through the glazed surface, allowing from ten to thirty per cent of the light in. These hi-tech *mashrabiyyas* are made up of 16,320 mobile modules; lozenges, squares, hexagons and circles combine to reflect and match the mosaic patterns of the floors of the IMA. The only element visible from the

FROM ABOVE: Since their installation, the only criticism voiced about the metal mashrabiyyas *has been the high cost of maintenance; octagonal, circular and square lenses precisely control the amount of light entering the library; OPPOSITE: The mechanical* mashrabiyyas, *which are a phenomenal technological update on the traditional wooden original, are a* tour de force; *OVERLEAF: The museum 'section' of the Institut; the view toward the Ile de la Cité and the Cathedral of Nôtre-Dame, linking two cultures*

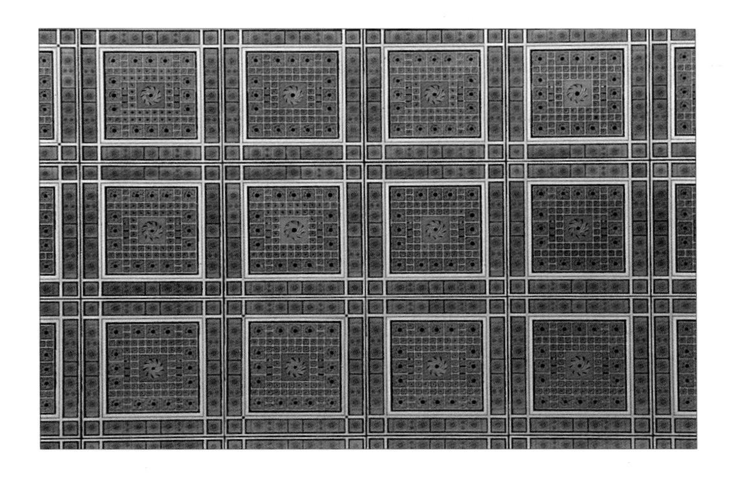

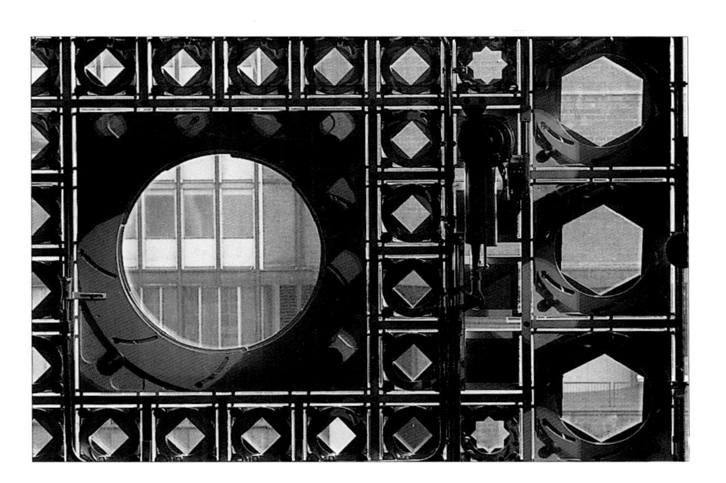

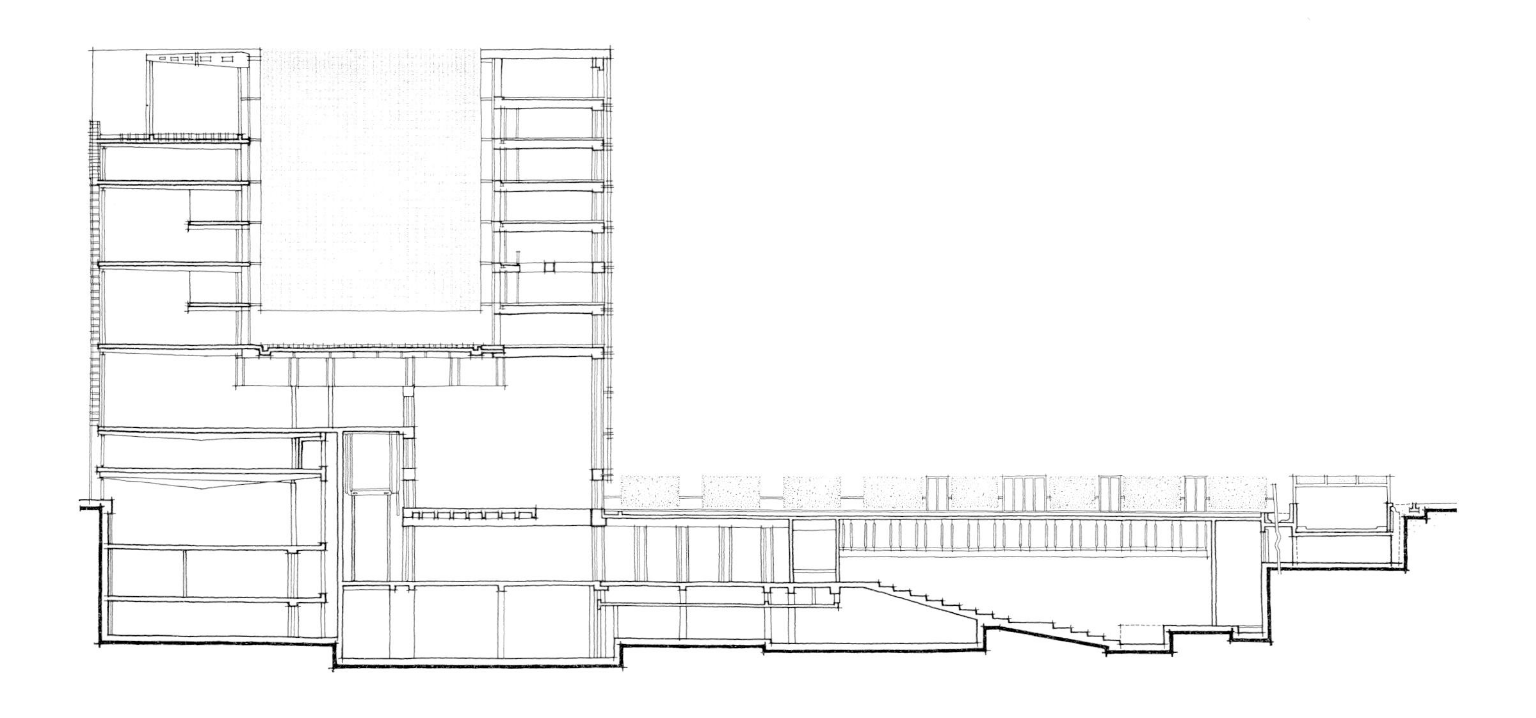

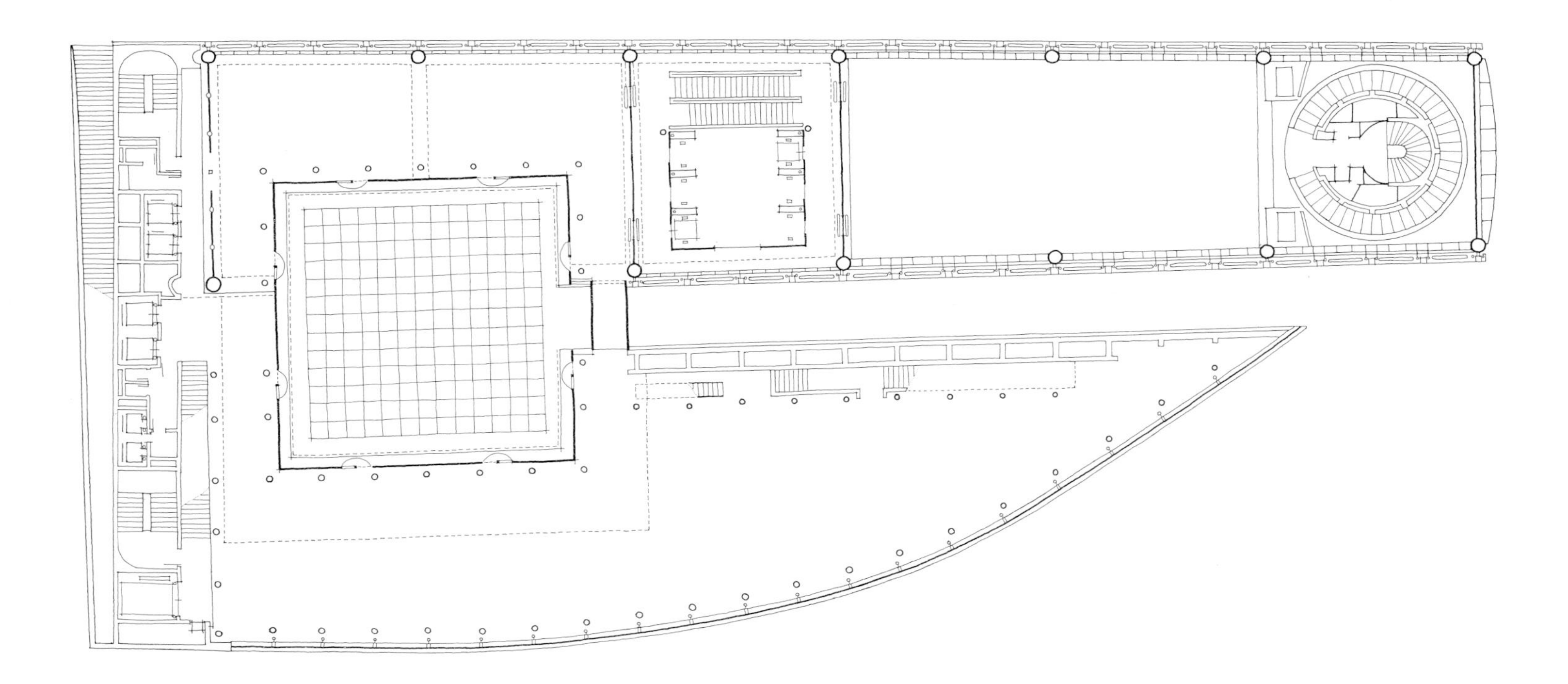

outside is the staircase tower of the library, which shines at night out to the boulevards.

The architect personified the role of the building in its exterior facades. The masked aspect of Islamic architecture, introverted, and hidden behind walls, is rendered here by the modern hi-tech curtain walls of aluminium, stainless steel and glass. Nouvel has said that he wants to 'forget the structure' of his buildings; here he hides it by a neutral, and modern skin which belies the reality inside.

The northern face of the IMA mirrors and reflects the Paris skyline, while the southern one conjures up the Arab World. Between these two worlds runs the slit which connects the inner court space to the outer one. The Islamic courtyard is symbolically linking up with the Parisian and Christian World, exemplified by Notre Dame across the river.

The site measures ten thousand square metres, but only 7,250 square metres were actually used for the ground and basement floors. The largest spaces are occupied by the Museum and Library, both 1,900 square metres, and the offices which take up 2,150 square metres. The services take up 7,290 square metres of space, the garage for 129 cars takes 3,350 square metres, and the terrace, square, court and ramp take 5,780 square metres.

The structural system is made of a steel frame with spans. Steel column, beams, trusses and secondary supporting elements support the curtain wall facades. These are made of glazed aluminium frames and tempered glass. Aluminium and glass are also the main materials used for interior partitions and doors. Ceilings, floor surfaces and the stairs are also metallic, and they are sometimes combined with plastic surface layers. The balustrade and elevator cage frames are also made of stainless steel and aluminium. Frameless glass elements, fixed by steel bracing wires, are used in the exhibition units of the museum. Marble is utilised for the pavement of the courtyard, while alabaster panels are used for some of the interior walls. The construction technology is completely industrialised and hi-tech; in fact it utilised the highest building technology available in France at that time.

The sophistication of the technological devices requires care and maintenance. Specialised firms were made responsible for the care of the mechanical and electronic equipment. A technical and maintenance network was organised to take care of the upkeep of the sophisticated materials used in the building, and this included the cleaning of the facades. So far all the systems seem to work quite well.

The IMA has very rapidly become a popular meeting place in Paris. It is frequented by many visitors who come to see the exhibitions, use the library, or just to see and wander about the building. They stroll on the terrace, use the cafeteria, or take photographs of Paris. These visitors are from diverse backgrounds. Although reactions to it are varied, they are generally positive. Most visitors agree that the formal aspect of its design integrates well with its urban Parisian setting, and that its elegant and dramatic use of hi-tech materials makes it a valuable addition to the architecture of Paris.

A survey conducted by Manar Hammad during one normal day elicited many interesting results. People were invited to express themselves freely on any subject connected to the building. The majority of visitors to the IMA that day were non-Arab and non-Muslim. Approximately eighty per cent of the people on the terrace, fifty per cent of the people in the exhibition, and forty per cent of those in the library were non-Arab and non-Muslim. For most of the visitors questioned, the IMA is not an Arab building, nor is it Muslim; it is simply an expression of French architecture. However, all Arab visitors seem to be very proud of the building. They appreciate its presence as a 'window open between the East and the West'. However, most visitors seem to think the building is too small and/or misuses its space.

The staff feel likewise. The transparent walls make privacy impossible. They feel enclosed in a small space with very low ceilings. All of them, librarians, museum keepers, and staff officers alike, feel they need more room for their projects. Although it appears large in photographs, in fact, the building is small in size. Visitors and architects alike expect it to be larger than it actually is.

The discrepancy in the reactions between the visitors and the users is dissipated by the fame that has come to the building. The prizes conferred on the building and the press and architectural accolades invariably influence people, and will transform their viewpoints.

High technology is what holds the IMA together. The volumes are simple, giving forth a message of restraint, a restraint based on understated wealth. It is in the rich quality of its materials and its finish that this building shines. Glass shines, and the surfaces of the aluminium shine. These shiny new qualities pervade the entire building, projecting a cool and perfect exterior facade. The IMA building appears to set a model for the Arab countries, not only in the technical field but also on the level of ideas, or goals to be achieved. No easy pastiche of Islamic motifs and designs is present in this building, no arches, no niches and no domes. The *mashrabiyyas* are used to explore geometric patterns, and are extraordinary technological innovations. Even when Nouvel uses the essential Islamic architectural idea of hiding a rich interior behind blank walls, he totally transforms it. His exterior facades reflect the outside world, and bring them into the interior spaces. It may be a message indicating the way for the future of the Islamic World.

OPPOSITE: Section; fourth-floor plan

The Significance of Cairo

JAMES STEELE

The international renown with which the cultural and historical heritage of Egypt is held centres around Cairo, because of the incomparable accumulation of Pharaonic, Graeco-Roman, Coptic and Islamic treasures that are located there.

Following the Muslim conquest of the Byzantine city in AD641, and the establishment of a military encampment called Al-Fustat, the governmental seat of the province of Egypt, as a critical part of the rapidly expanding Islamic Empire that was then being established, was continually enlarged by a succession of powerful ruling dynasties until it became the largest Muslim city in the Middle Ages, following the fall of Baghdad to the Mongol hordes.

At its zenith, Cairo was the centre of vast holdings that included Syria, Palestine, northern Mesopotamia and the Hijaz of Arabia with its Holy Cities of Makkah and Medina; and extended as far south into Africa as the Sudan. The first stage of this development was reached in AD870 when Ahmad Ibn Tulun declared his independence from the Abbasid Caliph and built his own enclave, called Al-Qatai, north of Al-Fustat. Nothing now remains of this settlement except his spectacular Friday Mosque, which now serves as a western point of demarcation for the city that was to follow. In AD969 the Fatamids, moving eastward along the Mediterranean coast of North Africa, established a city which they named Al-Qahira, 'the Victorious', which then became the nucleus of the medieval quarter. As Doris Behrens-Abouseif has explained:

> Under the Fatamids, Al-Qahira became the seat of power, a ceremonial residential centre where the Caliph dwelt with his court and army, but Al-Fustat remained the productive and economic centre of Egypt.[1]

She goes on to explain the way in which this has affected the name by which citizens recognise their city today by saying that:

> The word Cairo is derived from the Arabic Al-Qahira, which is not, however, the name commonly used by Egyptians to designate their capital. They have always called it *Masr* (the popular form of Misr, meaning Egypt) . . . Egyptian medieval historians make a clear distinction between Misr and Al-Qahira. The habit of calling the entire Egyptian capital Cairo, or Al-Qahira, was begun by Europeans who visited Egypt. The name was reinforced by Napoleon's French scholars, who made a survey of the city which they called Le Kaire, translated by the British as Cairo.[2]

The princely enclave which the Fatamids established was used as a base from which to challenge the authority of the Abbasids in Baghdad, making them a major power in the region. They set an architectural standard for all subsequent dynasties to follow, in the way that their significant monuments related to the urban context, which is a characteristic that now sets historic Cairo apart from all other cities in the Islamic world, because of the aesthetic standards that they applied. The Fatamid legacy, although regrettably reduced, is most evident today in the Al-Azhar Mosque and the University which they established with it, which quickly became renowned for setting the highest standards, as well as in the Al-Hakim, Al-Agmar and Salih Talih Mosques. The walls which they also built, and which have played such an important part in protecting the historic core from encroachment by the sprawling metropolis that continues to metastasise around it, were judiciously expanded by the Ayyubid Sultan Salah ad-Din, the 'Saladin' of epic legend. He used Crusader prisoners to complete the city gates called Bab en Nasr, Bab Al-Futuh and Bab Zuwaila, and to connect the two cities of Al-Fustat and Al-Qahira, with extensive ramparts that extended out to include the Citadel, where he transferred the seat of government in 1176.

Within these expanded boundaries, which encompass an area of nearly four square kilometres, the population of the city, which was inflated by refugees fleeing from uncertain conditions in the east, as well as by Salah ad-Din's decree that the princely enclave should be opened to all, and not reserved for the ruling class alone, forced changes in the linear, orthogonal structure, creating the twisting organic streets we see today.

Under the Mamluks, who ruled, in various forms between 1250 and 1517, this central core reached its height as a metropolis, since after the fall of Baghdad to the Mongols, the seat of the caliphate was transferred to Cairo in 1261, making it the political centre of Islam. Its wealth, due to its new status, and the monopoly it was able to establish on Red Sea trade, went into the construction of many large complexes, such as the extraordinary madrasa

and mausoleum of Sultan Qalawun, built between 1284 and 1285, which rivals the highest architectural achievements realised in Europe at this time.

Although the city did not regain this exalted position after the Ottoman Conquest in 1517, the momentum that had been established by that time continued, in the form of a conscious attitude toward the enhancement of an important legacy, and many fine architectural examples date from this period. A brief renewal of prosperity and power was achieved under Muhammed Ali; following the Napoleonic occupation of Cairo in 1798, and his rule, which was also administered from the Citadel, between 1805 and 1848, marked the final phase of the development of the historic core. The decision of Muhammed Ali to emulate European and especially French city planning techniques, and to open up vast new boulevards that moved outward to the north and west, is also significant, since it drew attention away from the centre, allowing Cairo to be spared the wholesale destruction suffered by other cities with such a distinguished historical legacy.

A succession of relatives that followed Muhammed Ali, namely his son Muhammed Saïd, his grandson Abbas, and his second grandson Isma'il, did not seem to share his capacity for leadership. With a few inspired exceptions, such as Abbas' decree of 1858, in which he renounced all governmental claims to ownership of land in favour of farmers who were allowed to both own land and pass it on after paying taxes on it for five years, the history of their rule is one of extravagance and increased borrowing from foreign banks, which took place in spite of unprecedented prosperity in Egypt, due to a shortage of cotton caused by the American Civil War during the rule of Isma'il Pasha. In his expressed desire to make Egypt, and Cairo in particular, 'a part of Europe', Isma'il spared no expense, and embarked on one ambitious project after another. These projects, as well as his own attempts to use financial inducements to wrest autonomy from the Sultan had consequences of staggering proportions. In the thirteen short years between his accession in 1863 and a declaration of national bankruptcy in 1876, the public debt had increased by three hundred per cent, which led to virtual foreign control of the country, lasting for seventy-six years, surviving two world wars and various nationalistic initiatives. The urban legacy of that presence is evident throughout Cairo, from the casual planning of Garden City to the more formal layouts of Mohandessin and Zamalek.

Demographic shifts, which characterise many countries in the developing world as they continue to assume more of the industrial burden that has now been bequeathed to them, are also affecting Egypt, as thousands move into Cairo from the countryside each month. The historic core, which was once home to a wealthy middle class of merchants, has now been overtaken by the rural poor.

The deterioration of the physical fabric, and the concomitant loss of services, in deference to more modern areas, has meant that the middle and upper middle classes have been supplanted. In their place a pattern of invasion-succession has now been firmly established by a transient population that has displaced established neighbourhood groups, who had a stake in their surroundings. While some members of this pre-existing group have retained businesses in the core, they no longer live there, meaning that a critical link in the symbiotic mixed-use cycle of residential shops that once made the area so viable, has been broken. Old buildings, which were once individually owned, and used by one family, have now been subdivided, and occupied by several, who typically live in severely overcrowded and unsanitary conditions. These greater densities have stretched the limited capacity of an ageing and neglected infrastructure, far past breaking point. The rise of the water table, due to inadequate sewer and drainage facilities, has radically accelerated the deterioration of the monuments in the area. As water rises through the stone by capillary action, it evaporates, leaving behind corrosive salts that cause the stone to crack. In some instances water marks as high as fourteen feet have been recorded on important buildings, and this will eventually cause the destruction of all decorative detail. In addition, air pollution related to increased traffic, which is growing at an average of ten per cent a year in the greater Cairo area, as well as pollution connected to rising industrial activity, has reached a critical level, aggravated by low fuel prices, which encourage its wasteful use.

The resulting threat to this unparalleled repository of Islamic heritage is now well known, and the choice of Cairo as the site of the 1989 Aga Khan Award for Architecture has done much to focus attention on this fact as well. It is hoped that initiatives, now underway, will succeed in reversing the forces which have combined to cause such destruction, and allow the historic core of Cairo to be preserved for many generations to come.

Notes

1 Doris Behrens-Abouseif *Islamic Architecture in Cairo: An Introduction*, American University in Cairo Press, 1989, p5

2 *ibid*, p6

FRONTIS: The mosque of Muhammed Ali dominates the skyline when approaching the city on Saleh Salem Street; OPPOSITE: Minarets were typically used in historic Cairo as visual points of reference, spaced at regular intervals

Contributors to the 1989 Awards

Steering Committee

His Highness The Aga Khan, Chairman
Dr Selma al-Radi
Professor Mohammed Arkoun
Professor John de Monchaux
Mr Hasan-Uddin Khan
Professor Charles Moore
Dr Ismaïl Serageldin

Master Jury

Dr Esin Atil
Mr Rasem Badran
Mr Geoffrey Bawa
Professor Charles Correa
Mr Kamran Diba
Professor Oleg Grabar
Dr Saad Eddin Ibrahim
Professor Hasan Poerbo
Professor William Porter

Technical Review

Dr Abdelhalim I Abdelhalim
Mr Jellal Abdelkafi
Dr Jamel Akbar
Dr Mohammad al-Asad
Dr Nur Altinyildiz
Dr Darab Diba
Mr Arif Hasan
Mr Romi Khosla
Mr Laszlo Mester de Parajd
Mr John Norton
Professor Serge Santelli
Mr Johan Silas
Dr Archibald Walls
Dr Atilla Yucel

Award Secretariat

Dr Saïd Zulficar
Dr Suha Özkan
Mr Jack Kennedy
Mr Farrokh Derakhshani